MY GOD
YOUR GOD
WHO?

This book is dedicated to my wife Iveta and my three Children whose lives make mine complete.

Iveta is the joy of my life, she is everything I could have wished for and everything I always dreamed of.

My son Daniel has always been my pride and joy and has grown into the sort of man of which any Father would be proud, kind, generous and conscientious.

My two daughters Carla and Casey are simply the most precious of children, full of joy, laughter and innocence. They are together the very centre of my life.

I am also very lucky to have two wonderful sisters Diana and Debbie whom I love deeply and whom have always been there for me when I have needed them and my brothers-in-law Rob and Jim who are both excellent men whose friendship I am lucky to have.

This book is then, dedicated to my family.

REV'D DAVID W. JOHN

MY GOD YOUR GOD WHO?

*A*dvantage
BOOKS

FOREWORD BY
THE RT REV'D NICHOLAS HOLTAM, BISHOP OF SALISBURY

My God, Your God, Who? by Rev'd David W. John
Copyright ©2021 by Rev'd David W. John
All Rights Reserved.
ISBN: 978-1-59755-630-9

Published by: ADVANTAGE BOOKS™ Longwood, Florida, USA

All Scripture quotations are taken from THE HOLY BIBLE, NEW INTERNATIONAL VERSION ®. Copyright© 1973, 1978, 1984, 2011 by Biblica, Inc.TM. Used by permission of Zondervan.

Library of Congress Catalog Number: 2021932888

First Printing: March 2021
21 22 23 24 25 26   10 9 8 7 6 5 4 3 2 1
Printed in the United States of America

Foreword

by the Rt Revd Nicholas Holtam, Bishop of Salisbury

Most of us put a lot of effort early on in life into working out what we believe and on what we can base our life. Sometimes things then happen that cause us to change our minds, modifying our assumptions and beliefs because of experience that doesn't fit with what we previously believed; or because something happens that causes a major discontinuity so that the old ways no longer work for us; or because we receive new information that brings light and shows us a better way, like St Paul on the Damascus Road where the world changed for him because of an encounter with Jesus Christ whom previously he had been persecuting.

The world sets the agenda of all serious theology. There is little point in the Church answering questions no one is really asking and producing an abstract and vacuous theology. What everyone seeks in life is meaning, life, love, friendship, community, purpose, goodness, truth, fairness and justice as well as how best to respond to the challenge of universal difficulties to do with our failures, guilt, suffering, sickness, death and grief. In all of this what if anything can be said and what lasts for ever?

Our world sees tolerance as a virtue and given the terrible things people have done to others in the name of God it is easy to agree. But it isn't enough to say if that's what you believe and it doesn't hurt anyone else that's OK. Good theology matters; bad theology is deeply damaging. Just look at the allegedly Christian myths in Section 1 that do such damage. We urgently need a positive account of what it is to be human that works for the common good and not just for my/our sectional interest. 'Love your neighbour as yourself' is a universal golden rule in all the world's religions.

'My God, Your God? Who?' is practical theology. David John has lived an interesting and full life. He has worked for the Metropolitan Police and for part of that time he has been a priest. Now no longer in the Police, he is a parish priest in Dorset in the Diocese of Salisbury, a very beautiful and mostly rural part of England. How does he connect his life and work with belief? He has faced life's complexities and tried to make sense of them in the light of his Christian beliefs.

David is one of life's natural teachers and wants to use his experience, insight, training and knowledge so that we learn with him. He wants to pass on his knowledge of Christianity and its wisdom. He has the enthusiasm, passion and energy of an evangelist who wants to share what he has found to be good.

There is an evangelical framework to this book in as much as this is good news being told by a passionate believer. David also makes the space for us to find our own response to what he gives us, to work out what we believe and make it our own, as each of us must do from time to time throughout our life. Here is belief you can base your life on. The electricity of the Christian faith comes when that which has been passed on to us by teachers is lived in real lives that are transformed by what inspires fidelity and is costly and sacrificial.

Jesus was a Jew and in Judaism a Rabbi is a teacher. Jews have a wonderful capacity for lively disagreement and finding the truth not so much in one person as within the community disputing and learning together through discussion. In this book David John is performing that sort of rabbinic role. He is contributing to a conversation which will be continued in the minds and hearts of those who read it and in the discussion of the groups that use it for their education. This is education that shapes the soul of individuals, families and communities.

David John says he has been working on this book for seven years but in reality it is the product of a lifetime. For all of us readers, I hope and pray it will help us to know, appreciate and explore Christianity and find in it the basis of belief that gives joyful life abundant and strengthens the common good.

Nicholas Holtam
Bishop of Salisbury

A Special Word of Thanks

I offer my very special thanks to The Rt Revd Bishop Nicholas Holtam the Bishop of Salisbury who has very kindly written the foreword to this book. I consider this a great honour. I was thrilled and not a little surprised when he agreed to support the publishing of this book.

I would also like to offer my sincere thanks to all those wonderfully talented theologians who taught me at Theological College, whose books I have read, commentaries I have dipped into and who have shaped my thoughts and understanding of theology over the past 40 years or so.

As I scan my bookshelf, I see such great minds as Donald Guthrie, R.T. France, Leon Morris, I Howard Marshal, and others, like all students of the subject I owe them a great debt.

In particular I would like to recognise and thank Dr Max Turner who was my New Testament tutor at the London Bible College (1983-85) (now the London School of Theology) and Professor of New Testament studies till his retirement in 2011 when he was given the title Emeritus Professor. There is no doubt that his New Testament studies course laid for me and many others the foundation for a lifetime of ministry.

Of all the 'Theologies' I have read the most influential for me has been George Eldon Ladd's Theology of the New Testament which I likewise discovered whilst studying at the now London School of Theology and devoured with joy.

I have used as a reference tool the free online encyclopaedia Wikipedia a truly excellent resource, my thanks to its contributors.

Over the years there have been some significant people who have supported me in a variety of ways who I would like to also thank, to whom I owe, what I would describe as a 'debt of love'.

From my days as a troubled teenager, Mr David and Maureen Mackay my first youth leaders, without whose love and support I would not have turned out to be the man I have become. From my early days as a young curate The Revd Dr Peter Galloway who guided me through my first years as my training incumbent. Most recently my Honorary Associate Priest (retired) Rev'd Garry Bennet and his wife Mrs Phyllida

Bennett their experience, generosity, and support here at the Iwerne Valley Benefice have been invaluable.

I should also finally offer my admiration and thanks to all those incredibly brave men and women who served alongside me over my 30 years as a London Metropolitan Police Officer who always 'had' my back and at times saved me from both personal injury or worse.

Table of Contents

Introduction

Before I launch into what can hopefully be described as a book on theology for the 'normal people of the Church', I thought it might be an idea to tell you all a little about myself by way of introduction.

I have in fact, wanted to write a book on theology for years but, if I am honest, I never really thought I was well educated enough to pull it off (having left school with just 3 'O' levels in English, Maths and Art.) and of course, it might well turn out that this effort is in fact quite inadequate.

I was born on May 15th, 1961 in Sevenoaks in Kent and so am now 59 years old. At the age of three my parents moved to Cardiff where I, with my two sisters, grew up.

My teenage years were a fairly dysfunctional and complicated affair, by the time I hit my teens my parent's marriage was disintegrating, my mother suffering badly from mental illness and my father although doing his best, was I suspect, rather overwhelmed by the whole situation. Life for me at this time was more often a case of surviving the stress and escaping from home rather than settling down to a solid education and blossoming into mature adulthood. All of which of course affected me greatly.

At 16 I became a Christian having been converted in what we might call the 'born again' 'Damascus Road' type fashion through the ministry of a youth leader at my local Baptist Church. I also, at about the same time embarked on the beginnings of my future career and joined the South Wales Police Force as a Police Cadet.

I 'grew up' then as a Christian in the Llanishen Baptist Church under the influence of an Evangelical theology with Charismatic overtones. I became a Youth Leader within the Church and after some time was recognised as someone with a calling to ministry. I found within the Church, during this period of my life, a replacement for the lack of a loving and secure home environment and threw myself into both my Faith and Church commitments with some vigour. It would be right to say that my experiences within the Baptist Church brought a degree of healing and restoration into my then rather fractured life, not least through the incredible commitment of Mr David and Mrs Maureen McKay the then youth leaders to whom I owe a debt which I suspect can never be fully repaid.

At 18 I joined the South Wales Police as a Constable trained at the Cwmbran Police Training College in Bridgend and was posted to the Canton Police Station in Cardiff in 1979 where I spent a very happy two or so years.

After being in the Police service for those two or so years I felt my first serious sense of call to the Christian ministry (in about 1982) so I left the Police and applied for Ordination into the Baptist Church. I went for an interview at Spurgeon's Baptist College; was provisionally offered a place for the following year; did a pre-course attachment for that year at Gillingham Baptist Church in Kent after which on failing an examination in New Testament Greek, Spurgeon's unexpectedly changed their mind.

Instead, I ended up studying for two years at the London Bible College (now the London School of Theology). My time at L.B.C. turned out to be fantastic; the theology I studied over those two years gave me a tremendous grounding for my coming lifetime of ministry.

After L.B.C. (and being a glutton for punishment) I applied for and was accepted onto an 'In Pastorate' training course at the Regents Park Baptist College, Oxford. I became the student Pastor of the Cricklewood Baptist Church in N.W. London, attending Regents Park College two days a week and thought that my future ministry was at last back on course. This again however did not go well; in 1987 the Baptist Church finally decided that they didn't want me after all.

This was perhaps the most difficult experience of my young life to date; I was utterly devastated; my world fell apart and I was also it has to be said, very angry and none too impressed with the way I had been treated by the Baptist College's.

Having no money, I luckily got a job labouring on a building site through the kindness of a chap whose wedding I had performed the same year. I took stock of my situation and decided to re-apply to the Police: This time in London.

I successfully joined the Metropolitan Police in London in 1988 and after the disappointments of the Baptist Church set my sights on this as my career for life.

The problem was, however, that despite these disappointments I just couldn't shake off my sense of calling to the Christian ministry. It was a torturous time as God continued to deepen my yearning for ministry. I joined another Baptist Church and after a while, I found myself 'inevitably' in ministry again becoming involved in a Church plant in Wembley N.W. London. Within a few months I was co-running this church plant with a young trainee Baptist Minister.

After about three years in this role my work circumstances changed which meant that I had to give up the Church plant in Wembley, I decided to leave the Baptist

Church and make a fresh start. I joined my Local Church of England Parish Church where I worshiped.

After about seven more years however, my sense of 'calling' to the ordained ministry was as strong as ever and through the help of my Vicar I discovered that I could become, what we call in the Church of England, a non-stipendiary or self - supporting Priest. I applied for that and thanks to God's Grace, I was accepted.

I trained part time whilst working full time in the Met Police and was Ordained in 2001 in St Pauls Cathedral. This was one of the most joyful and significant days of my life.

For the next three years I served as a Curate at the Emmanuel Parish Church West Hampstead under the wise guidance of the Revd Dr Peter Galloway and found myself experiencing a much more inclusive churchmanship. Peter is what we might describe as something of a Liberal Anglo-Catholic. The experience of working with Peter broadened my understanding of, not only ministry, symbolism and ecclesiology, but also gave me a deeper understanding of the miracle of God's grace and the wider ministry of the Holy Spirit. To say that working with Peter was transformational would not be to overstate his contributions to my churchmanship and spirituality. I am and always will be deeply grateful for my time at Emmanuel.

After those three years, in 2004, I became the Priest in Charge of St Cuthbert's Parish Church West Hampstead where I served until 2011 whilst still working nearly full time for the Met Police.

Whilst at St Cuthbert's I suppose I finally began to find my place as a Priest; my Churchmanship became a mixture of all my history and experience. I tried my best to blend together the elements of the Evangelical and Charismatic with the more traditional Church of England models along with a far greater appreciation of both symbolism and sacrament.

I came to believe deeply in the importance of liturgy but feel that within liturgy we must provide some space for people to engage with God in ways that sometimes words fail to allow. I am securely Evangelical in my understanding of theology, but I hope that within this I am not too narrow in my appreciation of wider theological positions. I believe in the centrality of both the Word of God faithfully taught and of the Sacramental ministry of the Church. I am a Charismatic in the sense that I believe in the presence, ministry and gifts of the Holy Spirit as an essential dynamic within all aspects of ministry whether liturgical or pastoral. Pastoral care is high on my priorities as a

Priest; I take the ordination 'gift' to me of 'The cure of Souls' very seriously. I feel deeply, it is ultimately what priestly ministry is all about.

My dreams of making St Cuthbert's a large thriving Church failed to come to fruition but we grew, doubled in size and had more adult confirmations in the 10 years I was there than in the previous 50. The congregation remained fairly small as we lost all our young adults every 2 years due to the cost of housing within N.W. London but in the end I felt that I left having done a reasonably decent job.

In 2015 I retired from the Police and found myself moving to Dorset to become the Vicar of the Iwerne Valley Benefice, a group of five rural Churches in the beautiful Dorset countryside. I have been here now for five years and have settled in well to a new ministry full of new challenges and so far, all seems to be going very well.

During these last 40 years or so I also got married, had a son, now aged 29, did various jobs within the Police service including Crime squad work, Robbery Squad work, uniform patrols, and murder investigations.

I divorced after an extremely difficult first marriage and in 2013 was lucky enough to get married again. My second wife Iveta is without doubt the greatest blessing God has ever given to me, we now have two beautiful daughter's Carla Ann aged 6 and Casey Rozalia aged 5 and they are a blessing to us both.

So here I am. The Vicar of the Iwerne Valley Benefice and at last, in full time ministry.

There is of course a lot more that could be said about the experiences of a retired 'veteran' serving Police Officer who is also a Christian and a Priest but that is not the purpose of this book. Maybe I will write another!

So why write a book on Theology?

A number of reasons I suppose.

Firstly, because there's so much rubbish around. Christian book rubbish I mean; you know the glossy soft covered paperback sort which you find in every Christian book shop written by those with huge agendas and even greater convictions of certainty. "Live the Victorious Christian Life" "Fire for Living" "The only Way" and other such titles are typical of the sort of books I mean. Books full of promise, victory, hope, certainty, power and success extolling how the truly charismatic writer already has these things and how we just haven't. Books explaining how we can find these things and have our lives and our experience of the Christian living transformed if we would only walk along their particular road. They want us to accept their teaching and embrace their particular theological formula which, in my experience, is usually based on some ill-conceived notion of the Bibles teaching on the Holy Spirit.

They are, what I call, the Christian "instant remedy books": Books which contain, so they say, the one remedy that will change your life. They are like diet books, and exercise workout videos, glossy, full of promise with beautiful people emblazoned all over them, sexy, provocative and very saleable. But, not for me, as you might have guessed, they simply smack of a sort of Christian propaganda, and just like the diet books and exercise videos, 90% of the time seem to solve little whilst promising so much.

I seriously doubt the depth of some of these writer's actual theological insight and expertise and I am often not at all convinced by the propositions they make based as they usually are on an erroneous view of the ministry of the Holy Spirit, a fundamental misunderstanding of true Christian discipleship and their own apparently amazingly successful experience of the Christian life, which they have then erroneously translated *into* the biblical text.

True theological reflection as we all know, comes from a different process, namely, the exposition of biblical truth from the biblical text within its context. Only then can such biblical truth be safely translated into our real lives as Christians peppered as they are with struggle, failure and compromise. I will myself within these pages attempt to "do" some such theology and hopefully I will avoid these same mistakes.

Now some of you may say "so what", why does it matter if the "Instant Remedy" books are misleading?

Well, it matters because, sadly, people believe them and those who struggle the most often believe them the most. They take the prescribed 'Christian super- pill' remedy in the hope of a cure and end up at best frustrated and at worst damaged when even after trying so hard to follow the rules they discover that nothing has really changed. They want to be victorious and successful, they want to live 'the Christian life of Faith' and are crushed again the first time they fail. Or alternatively they, having now found for themselves what they now believe is 'the cure,' fool themselves into believing that they have been in fact suddenly transformed and are miraculously now living this so called victorious Christian life, falling as they do, into a life of self-deception, self-righteousness and judgementalism. (*This is how you know, when Christians are subconsciously lying to themselves, they inevitably become defensive and start to look down on those whom they see as apparently less successful, frightened by those who are reflecting back at them their own true nature, from which they are hiding and from which they falsely and desperately want to believe they have been cured.)*

Theology then, is a powerful influence within the lives of Christians for good or for ill and should therefore not be taken lightly.

The second reason I have wanted to write this book is because I think I have something to say; something to help to address the confusion which seems to surround the lives of the Christians that I meet and minister too. I am not, as I have already said, much of a theologian. I don't even have a B.A. degree let alone an M.A. or Ph.D. and I fear right from the outset that those who do (should any ever read this) will point out all too easily the flaws and doctrinal propositions which would argue against my thoughts. However, I do think that I have a certain understanding of Faith and despite the above, a reasonably significant understanding of biblical theology. I hope too that I have a modicum of common sense and some insight into the human condition which, put together, might help to make what I say of relevance to some.

I have been a Christian for some 40 years now and have traversed the range of Christian thought and experience from the evangelical and Charismatic through the more Anglo-Catholic traditions and back to a sort of middle ground where my theology and spiritual experience embraces a fairly inclusive central position, at least I think so anyway!

I am a great believer in the work and presence of the Holy Spirit in our lives, and a greater believer in the truth that God is love and that he is far more concerned with our joy than we think he is and far less concerned with the failings of our humanity than we imagine he might be. Contrary to what many of us 'really think', Jesus did sort this all out on the cross 'once for all'. I hold firmly to the basic tenets of the Christian faith as traditionally understood by the mainstream Christian Church.

So why write a book?

Too dispel some myths, to offer some thoughts, to inject some truth into people's lives, and to see if I actually have anything useful to say.

So here we go:

Section 1

Myths

Over the years I have been a Christian I have been astounded at some of the things that other Christians believe both about the Christian Faith, the nature of God and about how he deals with us, his people. There seems to me to be three types of theology within mainstream Christianity; what the theologians teach; what we hear preached in our Churches and what individuals sometimes believe despite the former two. This third set of beliefs, at times, accord quite well with the traditional views generally expressed by the teachers, ministers and priests. At other times however they seem to develop within the minds of the congregations quite independently and often bear no relation at all, it seems, to that which is actually taught within the mainstreams of theological reflection. I call these third set of beliefs 'Folk Christianity' or 'Myths' and what troubles me mostly about these beliefs is not simply that they are often incorrect but that they are also often destructive and worst of all, often indelibly held within the psyche of individuals and impervious to debate or reason.

Why some Christians hold these particular views is complicated and has much to do, I think, with the sort of 'Bad Theology' as referenced in my examples above and also, very importantly what psychologists call our 'life scripts'. These subconscious 'scripts' or patterns of thought dictate how we see ourselves, others, the world, life, and if religious, our relationship with God.

Life scripts determine much of our lives, from the practical choices that we make to the subconscious view we hold of ourselves. We develop these 'life scripts' from the most powerful of influences, for example, from our relationships and in particular from those relationships that influence our early life, our parents, our childhood friends / associates, our schooling and perhaps in particular for Christians, from the faith beliefs we become exposed to during our most sensitive early and teenage years.

I also suspect that those of us who come to faith after our early teens tend to view our faith in the light of our *already developed* 'scripts' and use the experiences and teachings we are exposed to, to endorse the life scripts we already unconsciously hold. All of which is fine of course, if we are applying 'good scripts' to our faith beliefs, but incredibly destructive if they are bad.

If we felt that Daddy never really loved us and spent our lives trying to make him do so, for example, then when we come to faith we may subconsciously see God in that way too, embrace teachings that promote God as a judgmental God and thus never really feel accepted or loved by him.

Good theology is vital then not only because it can correct such damaging life scripts but also because it can help avoid our faith adding fuel to these destructive fires of negativity, which I suspect burn somewhere within many of us without us even knowing.

Folk Christianity then comes, in part, because of these psychological scripts and 'bad' theology is dangerous because it can become a tool used by us to justify our own damaged and negative view of ourselves. Likewise, it can be used by others to reinforce these negative subconscious beliefs for their own ends, a practice which some at last have come to recognise within the Church as Spiritual abuse.

As a possible example of this practice lets consider for a moment the following quote from the 1662 Book of Common Prayer call to Holy Communion:

'For as the benefit is great, if with a true penitent heart and lively faith we receive that holy Sacrament; (for then we spiritually eat the flesh of Christ, and drink his blood; then we dwell in Christ, and Christ in us; we are one with Christ, and Christ with us;) **so is the danger great, if we receive the same unworthily. For then we are guilty of (insulting) the Body and Blood of Christ our Saviour; we eat and drink our own damnation, not considering the Lord's Body; we kindle God's wrath against us; we provoke him to plague us with divers diseases, and sundry kinds of death.'**

In this call to Holy communion from the 1662 book of Common Prayer we find, without doubt, God portrayed as one who will enact a holy and cruel revenge on any who either refuse to attend Communion or who for one reason or another decide to take communion in an unrepentant (*unworthy*) state!! This is a prime example of a theology which promotes the idea of a wrathful God to be feared, rather than of the God, who in Jesus, we find PERFECT LOVE.

How, we should ask ourselves, could such an image of God contribute to the negative life scripts of those of us who come to faith with an already damaged view of themselves? And why indeed would the Church want, in the first place, to use this sort of 'emotional blackmail' to force people to attend Church and take Holy Communion?

Now, I have to add that when I read this at the 170TH anniversary of the rebuilding of St Bartholomew Sutton Waldron, the Church was packed with dozens of people from the village who I had never normally seen in Church and they all came forward for Holy Communion! But, regardless of this, is this sort of theology helpful? Are we right, in light of the teachings of the Cross (where Jesus apparently stood in our place, took upon himself the justified wrath of God for the sin of humanity and paid the price for all the sin of the world) to espouse such a fearful and wrathful view of God?

Thankfully we seemed to have moved on from this sort of image in most of our modern theological reflection. This then leads us to our first 'Myth' **'God still punishes us'.**

Myth 1: God punishes:

Life Script: "I am a bad person really and don't deserve forgiveness or real love"

Now, for most of us, consciously anyway, it might come as quite a surprise to find that many Christians still believe in a God who punishes them when they sin, but in my experience many do. They wrap this belief up in different ways for sure, but it is there. I met one Christian lady for example who had Chronic Arthritis in her hands. When I asked her about it and offered to pray for her healing, she maintained that there was no point as it was Gods punishment which he had visited upon her for a past indiscretion.

Others, for example, simply live with a sort of 'background fear' that God just doesn't quite love them. Some believe that God won't heal them because of their sin and others live on a perpetual quest to increase the amount that God loves them and so continually pray for forgiveness whilst forever trying, and of course failing, to live some sort of holier life.

All of these people, and others to varying degrees, live within a sort of spiritual 'limbo land' where the love of God is limited by their ability to earn it in some way or worse, where the love that God has for them has been corrupted by the way that they have lived their lives. For them, God stands above them holding out but not quite delivering his full cup of Grace, God withholds, God stands back like a Father who holds the cookie treat out while his baby toddler endeavours to stand up for the first time and walk over well enough to reach it for itself. When sickness comes it is God's punishment, "be sure your sins will find you out". When they are not healed it is because of un-confessed sin and when life goes wrong then they wonder 'who knows the mind of God". They comfort themselves with the belief that God knows why he has brought this on them or take on a belief that it must be for their benefit in some way: to refine their faith perhaps or to build their trust in him or they decide to accept a combination of such nonsensical rubbish in order to rationalise their suffering.

In the end, however, all this simply means is that God is a punishing God, punishing us: doesn't it? This is a view, as you might imagine, with which I cannot agree.

But what about the story of Job?

Good point, but really, even if we were to accept an interpretation of the Job story which appears to support a punishing God who ruins a poor man's life just to teach him a lesson or as part of a unique satanically initiated test. (There are other interpretations of course which by no means see the Job story in this way). Should we really build a whole New Testament post resurrection theology of suffering from this one story or any other Old Testament Story for that matter?

We must also ask ourselves whether with such a view, the Cross means anything at all? Can we really completely subvert the message of our Passover Lamb, Suffering Servant, Sacrificial offering, sin bearing Christ, in order to attempt to justify such a frankly perverse view of God, which in all likelihood has developed from our own inability to divorce our psychological life scripts from our experience and belief?

It might be interesting at this point to compare for a moment the example of the story of Job with Paul's teaching on Jesus as our High Priest found within Hebrews Chapter 4 and 5.

Hebrews 4:14-16 New International Version (NIV)

Jesus the Great High Priest

[14] Therefore, since we have a great high priest who has ascended into heaven, Jesus the Son of God, let us hold firmly to the faith we profess. [15] For we do not have a high priest who is unable to empathize with our weaknesses, but we have one who has been tempted in every way, just as we are—yet he did not sin.[16]Let us then approach God's throne of grace with confidence, so that we may receive mercy and find grace to help us in our time of need.

Firstly, it seems to me that the real message of the book of Job was to impress on his readers the fragility of life and the danger of investing one's hope and security solely within the temporal treasures of this world.

Secondly, to demonstrate to the readers the Almighty power of God in all things.

Thirdly to assure the readers of the healing power of God presence.

We should also very importantly, consider that it reflects the Old Testament belief that in the end everything comes from God. A belief similar to that contained within Islam, even today, where everything good or bad is assigned to the will of Allah; a theology which doesn't reflect the N.T. themes of human free-will and the ideas of the struggle that we face as Christians caught as we are, within the cosmic battle between Good and evil.

The overall picture of suffering within the Bible, I would suggest, does not reflect the belief that 'God causes suffering'. The NT picture rather sees suffering as a consequence of man's free will, the corruption of sin and portrays God now because of Christ, as the one who stands with us in love and compassion; as the one who stands as our companion and constant source of help within our suffering. This suggestion brings us nicely to our NT passage above. Jesus the great High Priest. What we have here in this quite incredible and wonderful passage is a description of how the experience of Jesus humanity has, in some way, transformed the person of God. How Jesus the divine Son, has through his experience of suffering and death enabled God the Father to become one who can now understand us, empathise with us and even suffer with us through the trauma's and temptations of our lives. I fully appreciate that any idea of God 'changing' causes all sorts of theological issues as to the perfection of God, his immutability, and all that sort of jazz. However, if God isn't capable of 'movement' of change within himself, of any sort of self-realisation, then how does he Love? How does he have compassion? How does God in fact have any emotion at all? As all emotion, at least as we understand it, involves a 'change' of direction, Paul says that we **were** enemies of God but that in Christ this all changed, now we are his friends, adopted as his children and so on! In the example of Jesus who is the image of the invisible God we see all sorts of decisions made and emotions in play! I leave the philosophical debate to those more qualified than me.

In our Hebrews' passage then, Jesus is selected by God the Father to represent humanity as our great High Priest within the person of God; to deal gently with us in our ignorance; to offer to the Father prayers and petitions on our behalf; to cry for us and to save us from death. In this picture from Hebrews, then, Jesus is sent to us by God the Father in order to become our advocate; to experience suffering, pain, the effects of sin, loss and death. He then takes these experiences back into God himself, creating by that journey out of the God-head and back into the God-head, a transformation within God.

God, by his nature cannot suffer or die because he is immortal, imperishable and everlasting, but in Jesus our great High Priest he has come to experience what it means for us to suffer and die. He can now share with us the pains that we go through and in this experience, we discover a deepening of the connection between God and us, a deepening of the eternal connection of Love.

The Hebrews' picture of God because of Jesus, is then, vastly different from the one portrayed in the Drama of Job.

No longer is God the detached chess board player moving his pieces around in order to win the game, he is the loving, feeling, compassionate Father, suffering in love with the children he created. He is the one who listens to their cries and to the cries of Jesus and who provides them with salvation through his Son.

No longer is he the God of Judgment to be feared, but the God of love whose throne in heaven we can now approach with boldness and confidence.

No longer is he the God who rages at Israel because of their sin and disobedience, he is the God who in Jesus has wiped those sins away.

No longer is he the God who replies to our complaints asking "who is this who dares to approach me", he is the God who opens his heart to us, embraces us and welcomes us home. He is all these things because Jesus has come; because Jesus has suffered, because Jesus has died for us and paid the price for our sins. Jesus stands within the God-head pleading for us, because in the humanity of Jesus, in his suffering and death God experiences with us the tragedy of our humanity, our suffering and our pain.

14 Therefore, since we have a great high priest who has ascended into heaven, [a] Jesus the Son of God, let us hold firmly to the faith we profess. 15 For we do not have a high priest who is unable to empathize with our weaknesses, but we have one who has been tempted in every way, just as we are—yet he did not sin. 16 Let us then approach God's throne of grace with confidence, so that we may receive mercy and find grace to help us in our time of need.

So, come to God with this confidence... because we are accepted.

Come to God with hope... because we are forgiven.

Come to God if you are weak and sinful... because we have Jesus with us and before us, our great high priest, pleading our case and we have a God who understands, who embraces, who accepts and who now suffers with us.

In the new era, post Christ's life, death and resurrection, God isn't ever portrayed like a father 'tempting us' with the promise of his love. God IS Love, at least that's what the New Testament tells us! God LOVES us absolutely and completely. As for his wrath, according to my Bible that was completely satisfied on the Cross at Calvary. As far as my sins, he sees them no more. He has poured out his grace upon us; he doesn't hold anything back and in Christ we are completely acceptable in his sight. This IS the message of the Gospel, "there is no punishment left for sin"!

Any other teaching, and all those desperate attempts to see God as one who either punishes us or withholds his love until we are better people simply deny the efficacy of his work in Christ and so they must be wrong! mustn't they?

It must be right then, surely, to assert that God does not punish us! He never brings upon us illness or suffering, pain or hurt; he never withdraws from us because of sin, any sin. He, if anything, holds us tighter in these times less we fall away from him through our own sense of unworthiness! This IS the Gospel of Christ.

A short aside

Have you ever wondered, by the way, *why* anyone would teach this sort of theology? That is, a view of God which makes him a God to be feared?

As a minister, wouldn't that give someone a very real sense of power and control over his /her flock? After all, if God is like this and you are his authoritative messenger and 'the voice of his wrath', where does that place you?

I would seriously question the hidden motives and life scripts behind any Christian leader who taught in this way, especially if he/she seemed themselves to be presenting a self-image of the ideal example of Christian discipleship.

Myth 2: God is in control.

Script: I need to feel that someone else controls my life because I have never learnt to deal with responsibility, uncertainty or insecurity.

Now of course this is a bit of a biggie I know and one that has dogged the modern church since at least the teachings of Calvin. Gods control verses man's free will; omnipotence against impotence, chance as opposed to divine intervention.

The two opposing positions, as I see them, put in the most basic of terms state this:

- On the one side - God's sovereignty is unconditional, unlimited, and absolute. All things are predetermined by the good pleasure of God's will.

- On the other side, - Gods control over the universe and our lives is limited in correspondence with man's freedom and response. Our experience of life results from the decisions and choices that we make along with a random collection of chance events. We as Christians and non-Christians alike therefore live, to some extent, at the mercy of what life brings us. The message of the Gospel within this view is that within this 'universal situation' God acts continually to redeem both our world and us, as individuals, from the consequences of our failure and sin and has ultimately done so in Christ.

Sounds a simple choice doesn't it but of course it isn't. Each set of beliefs brings with it huge definitions about the nature of God himself. In the end, we simply can't separate 'who God is' from that which we perceive him to do or allow, or not do, particularly if we see Gods inaction as an action of choice. There is no easy answer to the problem. So why do I so definitely assert that the statement "God is in control" is a Myth?

Simply because in my view he can't be!

The starting place for this discussion comes from two separate positions firstly from the nature of God as revealed in the New Testament and secondly from the nature of the world around us.

This isn't to suggest by the way that God won't sort all things out in the end or that the eventual destiny of all things will not be subject to his design. In the end, I believe that God will redeem the universe and triumph. No, what we are discussing here relates to the everyday situations within both our lives: more broadly the events within human history. This proposition doesn't claim to answer all the questions; the fact is that none of the arguments work completely, mine simply makes more sense to me. So:

Christians who believe that 'God is in control' hold a number of variations on the theme and apply these views to human life in different ways. At its most extreme God simply controls everything that happens physically within the world. Furthermore, proponents of this view also attribute God's control to the question of salvation, believing in what some call the theology of 'double predestination' in which God's control over mankind is so complete that he even chooses not only those who will come to salvation in Christ but also actively chooses those who won't and who are therefore condemned to Hell.

The problems with this (more extreme) view are of course obvious. Firstly, man has no self-determination, no real choice or free will. Secondly, God becomes the one who selects (on some unknown basis) who will be condemned for all eternity! God then becomes the destroyer of men; the torturer of humanity both in this life (as he predestines suffering) and for eternity. For most Calvinists in my experience also believe in an eternal hell of millions of human souls. Furthermore, those whom *you* have the capacity to love as a mere flawed human being (if this person is not chosen to be saved) is to be unloved for eternity by the God who apparently is Love! The contradictions are too much for me.

Other Christians hold perhaps a lesser view of God's control but nevertheless tend to see pretty much everything as in some way pre-ordained, including the choices that we make within our lives.

Of particular interest to me within this circle of beliefs is the observation that, in my experience, people who hold these views seem to place a particular emphasis on God's control of all the things that go wrong for them. A fact that I have always found to be frankly a bit odd. Such Christians are for example, really 'happy' to attribute all their tragedies and traumas to God's divine will while on the other hand, and equally as confusing, seem to take the good things in their lives as some-how less than the result of God's blessing. I need to perhaps clarify a little of what I mean by this. It isn't that these Christians don't see the good things as from God, but the ***emphasis*** they place on Gods control of the good events seems some-how less intense. In suffering, their faith intensifies as they use their theology of God's omnipotence to construct a more cope-able framework in which to survive their obvious pain.

One may think for example, of such people as 'Joni' who wrote a book in the 70's which became a most famous Christian bestseller. Joni dived into the sea when she was a young girl and broke her neck. She was paralysed and spent her life inspiring others through her belief that God had caused this to happen to her in order that she might preach the Gospel, exemplifying as she did, an example of true suffering and yet victorious spirituality! Now I have no doubt at all, that during this horrendous situation God acted, God ministered and God redeemed her situation so that her wonderful ministry developed, but to say that God caused the accident in order to do this seems perverse to say the least.

Ultimately these in my opinion erroneous views, seem to come from *probably* two different sources. Firstly, from our life scripts and secondly from our monotheistic (there is only one God) theology. In particular this second point, I would suggest, comes from the very distinctive monotheism of the Old Testament where it has to be admitted God's all-encompassing omnipotence has a very high standing and where everything is certainly seen as coming directly from God. The proposition: 'There is only one God whose divine will must therefore governs all things' is the proposition in question here, but, in reality, does it? While those who wrote the Old Testament may have culturally followed this idea does such thinking stand up today against the revelation of God held in Christ and within the pages of the N/T?

I don't think it does.

Is God the author of our sufferings? Does he bring them into our lives for some unknown divine reason, to teach us lessons or to refine our faith? Personally, I don't see this at all. After all, why would he? If he wanted to teach us these lessons why would he do so in the cruellest of ways? And where does it stop? Is personal tragedy, national tragedy, suffering and pain actually Gods will at times for our lives? As a Police officer I saw countless acts of evil perpetrated on people by other people. Are these victims supposed to see God as in some way the *motivator* behind these events? In my view this simply makes no sense at all. It makes our N/T God of love into an evil despotic ruler who simply toys with his creation inflicting needless suffering supposedly to achieve his own ends.

I prefer a more fluid theology.

For me life is a mixture of the random and of what we make it. It is determined by circumstances, by choices made sometimes by ourselves and sometimes by others and we should add, from the consequences of a powerful evil that has entered our existence and which corrupts all creation.

God, I believe, seeks constantly by his grace, to redeem life and bring into our lives the power of his healing Christ centred Love as revealed in the Gospel.

I will expand my view:

Theologically, I would suggest, we live in a world that since the fall exists in a state of 'Chaos', in a state of decay. The universe is dying, falling apart if you like, spiralling downwards, all is not set or part of some carefully worked out plan or working as it should be and this biblically speaking is the effect of a disease called sin.

The results of sin are firstly, all that is bad in the world, secondly, the presence of a significant spiritual evil and thirdly the selfishness that exists within the hearts of both men and women which also corrupts our lives and the lives of others.

In the New Testament this current state is illustrated perhaps most strikingly in the Apostle Paul's concepts of the 'new verses the old order.' In a variety of different ways Paul talks of a tension between what God is doing through the new ministry of the kingdom in Christ and the 'old corrupted order/situation/world' in which the whole universe exists.

In the new kingdom (the places where God's kingdom influence is now active) God is working to bring redemption, that is, he is present and active and working to bring peace. God then, provides us through this, a foretaste of what is to come when he will act to re-create all things. God is not then in control, at least not yet, (we kicked him out in the garden of Eden) but he is here and his presence brings into our lives the influence of his redemptive action and love by the power of his Holy Spirit and in Christian terms anyway the place where this influence is most active and obvious is called his Church.

In his Church universal, in its people, in their lives and through its ministry to the wider world God exerts his influence and seeks to deliver to all a foretaste of his new Kingdom and of his love. His role then, if you like, rather than being to control (for the world is lost to him by its own choice) is to redeem, to make good from that which is in chaos, to bring some order and love to that which is in decay, to quote Paul "God works IN ALL THINGS for good for those who love him". This is my view.

In practical terms then when tragedy comes it is neither God who brings it or who orders it, it is part of life and a direct consequence of the fact that life, existence itself, is in chaos. It is a result of sin, of man's inability to live as God had intended. It is the result at times simply of the decisions of evil people, of the influence of this corruption within mankind itself. It is also, I believe, the result of spiritual evil an independent force which exists in opposition to God and whose aim is to corrupt all that is good. The bible calls the author of these influences the Devil or Satan.

God's role within this universal tragedy is then, as I have said, to redeem. If we let him he will come along side us, love us, deliver us, reassure us and give us hope even within our darkest moments, for Christ has conquered all darkness and even death itself, the ultimate loss.

In conclusion then to say that God is in control denies his nature for HE IS LOVE. It also denies the fact of man's free will and flies completely in the face of reality itself. There is simply too much badness, sadness, and evil in the world for it to be true.

Does this make God powerless? Not at all, for he is redeeming all things.

Isn't this in itself a bit mean? Why doesn't God step in and change things? He has and he is in Christ.

Why did God let all this chaos exist in the first place? Why did he let man fall into sin and let sin corrupt the world? Why didn't he create without the possibility of corruption?

Perhaps because free will is an essential aspect in creation. To create without the possibility of that creation failing, without giving it the ability to be creative itself (with all the dangers that brings) would perhaps make creation itself pointless. Also, of course, we tend to think that God is limited by nothing but perhaps he is limited by his own very nature, perhaps God 'HAD' to create in this way? Does God have the ability to act outside of his nature? I don't think he can for to do so would cause him to deny himself (or in other words, to sin, and if there is one thing God can't do, its sin.) So maybe this is just the way it had to be! Creation had to have the choice and sadly it chose to sin, to follow its own path and by doing so brought all this chaos into the world as it fell away from God and automatically began to die.

The Grace and love of God is shown in the fact that while we, like the prodigal son, walked away and squandered our inheritance, God followed us and has been loving us back to himself within the chaos ever since and despite our rejection of him.

Myth 3: God's ability to bless us can be limited by our failures.

Script: I am never good enough to receive God's full blessings

As with our first 'Myth' many readers might seem surprised by the suggestions contained in the third Myth. After all we believe that God is all powerful, all knowing and of course the master of his own decisions and will, don't we? To suggest then that God could be constrained in some way by human beings seems ridiculous, but I have heard it taught nevertheless and most often, in my own experience of the Church, within the context of the Christian healing ministry. This will then be, by way of an example, the context for this discussion.

There is then amongst some Christians of the Charismatic persuasion (of which I am one) the belief that, if you are sick, God automatically wishes to make you better.

This belief stems from a number of theological pre-suppositions which are usually.

1. That God wants to heal because all our infirmities were carried away by Christ on the cross (a theology developed from the Old Testament prophet Isaiah's description of the 'Suffering servant')

2. That God wants to heal us of all sickness because he wants us to have what the New Testament calls 'abundant life', (a fundamental misunderstanding of what Jesus meant by this expression, see later chapters).

3. Because sickness is a part of the afore-mentioned 'Old order' which in this view has been completely overtaken, (within the lives of Christians anyway) by the presence of the new Kingdom of God, (a misunderstanding of Jesus teaching on the Kingdom, see later chapter).

4. Because some (Charismatic Christians) have a mistaken tendency to see miracles as an end in themselves (a point I will look at and explain in a moment).

The problem with holding this sort of view however comes naturally when God doesn't heal (which of course, if we are honest, covers most situations most of the time). In my experience real healings are relatively rare. When this happens (when healing doesn't come to the sick person) the struggle begins to find out *why* and usually various explanations are offered revolving around this belief that we are in some way limiting God's abilities to bless.

Some, under these circumstances, attribute the 'non-healing' to the belief that the victim must have un-confessed sin in their life adding guilt to the sufferings of the already sick! Or:

To the possibility that 'we're not praying with enough faith, making both the sick and the ministers praying, guilty! Or:

To the belief that God has withdrawn from the particular situation and is punishing the sick person because of past indiscretions (well, just ludicrous, see above) and in some cases because "we've forgotten the holy oil" (well really!)

In each of these scenarios, three massive assumptions are being made:

Firstly, that God's role within the world actually includes, at this point in his kingdom plan, the healing of all our sicknesses (which by the way would ultimately and logically mean that we would never die!)

Secondly, that God is being frustrated / limited by us!

Thirdly, that the physical healing of sickness is and was in Jesus own life an end in itself, that when Jesus healed there was no context or reason for doing so <u>outside of</u> the benefit received by the person healed. (A mistaken assumption which in my view misses the point of Christ's healings altogether).

The first assumption: '*That God wants to heal because all of our infirmities etc were carried away by Christ on the cross*'. This belief is based on a misunderstanding of Christ's own 'Kingdom teaching', a misunderstanding battled out years ago between the theologians Weiss and Switzer.

One taught that the Kingdom of God had arrived IN ITS TOTALITY through Christ's ministry, (inferring that all the kingdom blessing's had arrived in full as well) the other taught that it was ALL YET TO COME, that the Kingdom (and its blessing's) would arrive <u>only</u> at the end of time when God would act to re-create the universe.

Neither of these two chaps were in fact right of course. What Jesus actually taught was that the 'coming' of the kingdom was a *process* which although started in him and his ministry would not conclude until the end of days.

In Jesus' teachings the kingdom starts and then grows like a mustard seed or like a bit a yeast in some dough (see the parables of growth in Jesus teaching and you get the picture). Logically of course, I would suggest, the same applies to the 'benefits' of the kingdom. They, like the kingdom itself, have come 'in part' as a 'foretaste' of that which is to come, thus the possibility of physical healing has arrived but to assume that God wants everyone to be healed all the time assumes a role for God which he has yet to initiate. We will all be healed of course one day, but at the end of days when the kingdom and all its benefits arrive in full, or as Jesus might have put it "when the tree is full grown," when God restores all things etc.

There are, of course, within this initial period of the kingdom's presence certain 'eschatological' (end time) benefits which have arrived in their fullness e.g. forgiveness, but these are the exception by Gods Grace and what's more are clearly taught as having arrived in their fullness within the teachings of the New Testament.

The second assumption is that God is limited in what he can or can't do by us, perhaps by our sin or by our lack of faith.

To me this seems again to be just a bit silly. I know there is that one example where the Gospel writer tells us that Jesus performed no miracles in one town because they had no faith, but again (as with the Job thingy) can we really build a whole theology of 'God being limited by man" on the basis of one decision that Jesus made in one situation? Surely if this was a major theological consideration, if Jesus or the N/T writers had seen this as a major problem, then the New Testament would be full of warnings about it!

Also, we should note, that in most cases when Jesus or the first disciples healed, the person's faith seemed to have little, if any bearing at all on the miracles performed.

Take the healing of the beggar outside the temple gates by Peter in Acts. This was the first post resurrection healing. The beggar didn't even know of whom he was asking for money. Peter doesn't spend hours counselling him on his need for faith prior to the miracle. The man wasn't even a Christian at the time, Peter just reaches down, tells him that he has no gold or silver and commands him to get up and walk!

Or take for example Christ's own healings. On one occasion Jesus tells a cripple that his sins are forgiven and then heals him purely in response to a challenge by the Pharisees who doubted his right to forgive sins! In this case Jesus' healing has nothing at all to do with the man's faith or for that matter his sickness and everything to do with proving to a disbelieving crowd the nature of his own person. Our ability to have a strong enough Faith then seems irrelevant.

We should also on this point remind ourselves of the argument above about God's love. Knowing as he does, that we are weak, if God really wanted to heal all of us of everything then would such a loving God just walk away from us and condemn us to continued suffering just because we are scared, hurting and broken? Please say no.

This leaves the suggestion that God doesn't heal because of un-confessed sin!

To this I would ask three questions.

1. Do any of us actually remember or even know ALL our sins?

2. Are we suggesting here that un-confessed sin stops God working and if so, are these then the sins that God forgot to deal with on the Cross?

3. Do we really believe in a God who would punish us as well as Jesus?

Isn't the WHOLE POINT of the cross denied by such a suggestion? This idea is of course then non-sense and seems to completely contradict the teachings of scripture at its most basic of levels.

Finally, were Jesus healings an end in themselves?

The suggestion that God wants to heal us all, all the time, also seems to presume that physical healing from illness was for Jesus an end in itself, that there was no other motive for the miracles other than the well-being of the person so healed. ***So why did Jesus heal people?*** And why did this manifestation of the Kingdoms presence post Easter, continue to be a part of the early disciple's ministry?

If Jesus healed as a direct result of his overwhelming love and simply to make people better or if it was the natural and automatic consequence of the kingdoms presence, then one can see how some would come to believe that it should, if the kingdom is truly present in our lives, continue to happen automatically today, however what if Jesus reasons for healing people were different? What if his motive behind them was specifically something else? How would this help us to place the whole complicated question of healing today in a clearer context?

Well for an answer let's go back to the examples above; why did Jesus heal the crippled man? Answer: In order to silence the doubting Pharisees, in order to prove that he had the authority to forgive sins or in other words in order to prove that he was Divine / the messiah.

The motive was then evangelistic.

In regard to the first post-Easter miracle by Peter, if you read the context it is clear why the miracle happened. After he was better the formerly crippled man ran through the Temple courts praising God. Those seeing him questioned Peter and John who, of course, yes you've guessed it, used the miracle as the means of preaching CHRIST AS MESSIAH. Miracles, then perhaps, have much less to do with the people who benefit from them and everything to do with EVANGELISM! They are perhaps better understood as the visual aids for the Gospel.

Miracles were then, visual aids for Jesus and for the Early Church and I would suggest that when God heals today it is most likely to be for the same reasons. He heals when he wants in order to advertise the truth of his Gospel to an un-believing world (or to encourage his church to a greater faith) and this historically is perhaps why miracles always accompany revival but don't always accompany the day to day living of the Church.

For those who aren't healed then we need to remember two things, firstly, that sadly we are all a part of a decaying existence, brought about by our universal abandonment of God. Our current sufferings are a direct result of this situation. Secondly and most importantly, that regardless of this God in Christ offers us an eternal hope because he is restoring all things including us to perfection. He is redeeming his world and when the kingdom does come in its fullness, we will all live forever and in that perfection. We will be healed; we will be restored and from the perspective of eternity the suffering we suffer today will be as nothing. God really does love us.

So then, to suggest that the blessings God wishes to bestow upon us can be limited by us as individuals or by the Church seems to be wrong. God has and is intervening within our history and within our lives in and through Christ in the ways he chooses. His primary purpose is to bring us hope love and eternal peace and to promote the truth of the Gospel message through which all men and women can, in the end, be completely healed and saved.

Myth 4: God dislikes some people and loves others.

Script: 'I am better than them and I deserve more'

A tricky one this, after all, **we all like some people more than others** don't we! It would make sense to me that God would likewise feel less inclined towards a murderer than he does towards a member of the Peace core.

The problem with this idea however is that according to my reading of the Bible it appears that as far as being good or not God see's us all as equally lost in our sinfulness regardless of our lives, position, status or even behaviour and the only thing which appears to alter this view at least in terms of our standing before him is our response by faith to the Cross and resurrection.

It is only faith in the Messiah then which creates any distinction, placing some of us within Gods incredible grace. Without such faith we, it seems, all remain equally the objects of God's wrath.

Romans chapter 1.

God's Wrath Against Sinful Humanity

[18] The wrath of God is being revealed from heaven against all the godlessness and wickedness of people, who suppress the truth by their wickedness, [19] since what may be known about God is plain to them, because God has made it plain to them. [20] For since the creation of the world God's invisible qualities—his eternal power and divine nature—have been clearly seen, being understood from what has been made, so that people are without excuse.

Now, from one perspective, of course this is wonderful news because it is within the grasp of all people to be saved. On the other hand however, it also demonstrates the fact that without faith we are all seen as equally corrupt, a fact which is more difficult to grasp and one that many of us at times seem to conveniently forget when we wish to 'do our fellow human beings down'.

The issue here then is '**how do we as Christians** see each other within the diversity which is human nature?' And why, when we survey our fellow human beings, do we find ourselves judging others as less than ourselves?

The answer seems to me to do with our own moral conditioning. We are conditioned to 'judge' each other, and we make these moral judgments in reference to the norms and standards of the communities in which we live.

In most countries including the U.K. we, generally speaking, start our judgments of right and wrong by reference to the law of the land. After this we then tend to develop further moral positions based on our understandings of a wider morality refining our opinions of others based on our own personal values which we have developed from the various 'communities' to which we have been exposed, our families, our culture, our education and so on, all of which is normal and fine.

In the Church for example, we join and discover a 'new', what we might call 'mini community', and as Christians, then become 'morally conditioned' by our faith beliefs which refine our judgments of right and wrong based on the culture and teachings of our new Church.

Our community and 'sub' or 'mini' communities, whatever they are, then condition how we see our fellow human beings. Again, this is quite the normal way of things, we all do this.

The problem with all this, however, is that such 'community conditioning' is completely random. For example, in the 'new sub or mini Community' of a Prison where the majority of people are criminals, 'normal' criminals are the acceptable residents, whereas in my experience as a Police officer, sex offenders and paedophiles are the unacceptable! I can also say from my own experience of the criminal world that within the 'sub community' of criminality, it is considered morally OK to be a criminal! Criminals can justify most criminal activity up to a point without any issues. Also amongst a community of sex offenders for example, sex offending is justified and acceptable: You only need to interview a sex offender to discover how some of them will, and with a sense of ease, justify who they are and the way they have behaved. Whereas of course, within the larger general community these behaviours are condemned. On a different level, in the 'vegetarian / vegan community' at its most extreme, those who eat meat are considered to be murderers!

The point is that for us as Christians we need to understand that when we do judge our brothers and sisters we are judging them in reference to, firstly, the general community within which we live, and secondly, by the way that we have been conditioned by our own 'sub' or 'mini' communities. Then again by the Christian 'standards' that we have been exposed to since we became Christians and joined the 'mini' community of the Church. We need to understand that because of this, our judgments are in no way guaranteed to reflect the actual mind of God, which is perhaps why Jesus counselled so convincingly against the practice.

Matthew 7:1-5

"Do not judge, or you too will be judged.²For in the same way you judge others, you will be judged, and with the measure you use, it will be measured to you.

³"Why do you look at the speck of sawdust in your brother's eye and pay no attention to the plank in your own eye? ⁴How can you say to your brother, 'Let me take the speck out of your eye,' when all the time there is a plank in your own eye? ⁵You hypocrite first take the plank out of your own eye, and then you will see clearly to remove the speck from your brother's eye.

Further to this, in Biblical terms, what we also need to recognise is that the only 'community' by which we should judge our goodness and the sin of others is the Community of God himself, which as we know is a community of perfection. Which brings me I hope, nicely, to my point.

If our point of reference for judgment is, and only is, the community of God's perfection, then we can begin to see clearly why the Bible calls us to recognise the equality of our condition.

No One Is Righteous

Romans 3

⁹What shall we conclude then? Do we have any advantage? Not at all! For we have already made the charge that Jews and Gentiles alike are all under the power of sin.

¹⁰As it is written: "There is no one righteous, not even one; ¹¹there is no one who understands; there is no one who seeks God. ¹²All have turned away, they have together become worthless; there is no one who does good, not even one." ¹³"Their throats are open graves; their tongues practice deceit." "The poison of vipers is on their lips." ¹⁴"Their mouths are full of cursing and bitterness." ¹⁵"Their feet are swift to shed blood; ¹⁶ruin and misery mark their ways, ¹⁷and the way of peace they do not know." ¹⁸"There is no fear of God before their eyes." ¹⁹Now we know that whatever the law says, it says to those who are under the law, so that every mouth may be silenced and the whole world held accountable to God. ²⁰Therefore no one will be declared righteous in God's sight by the works of the law; rather, through the law we become conscious of our sin.

Righteousness Through Faith

²¹But now apart from the law the righteousness of God has been made known, to which the Law and the Prophets testify. ²²This righteousness is given through faith in[b] Jesus Christ to all who believe. There is no difference between Jew and Gentile, ²³for all have sinned and fall short of the glory of God, ²⁴and all are justified freely by his grace through the redemption that came by Christ Jesus. ²⁵God presented Christ as a sacrifice of atonement,[c] through the shedding of his blood—to be received by faith. He did this to demonstrate his righteousness, because in his forbearance he had left the sins committed beforehand unpunished— 26 he did it to demonstrate his righteousness at the present time, so as to be just and the one who justifies those who have faith in Jesus.

27 Where, then, is boasting? It is excluded. Because of what law? The law that requires works? No, because of the law that requires faith. 28 For we maintain that a person is justified by faith apart from the works of the law. 29 Or is God the God of Jews only? Is he not the God of Gentiles too? Yes, of Gentiles too, 30 since there is only one God, who will justify the circumcised by faith and the uncircumcised through that same faith. 31 Do we, then, nullify the law by this faith? Not at all! Rather, we uphold the law.

In the passage above Paul the Apostle is clearly negotiating in this way with the Roman Christians because they have been judging each other on the basis of their nationality e.g. Jew v Gentile, they are judging each other then, on the basis of their own 'sub' or 'mini communities' conditioning, just as we do today and as we can clearly see, by doing this, they are missing the point of God's salvation completely.

We cannot then and should not look down in judgment on our fellow brothers and sisters based on the morality of our own 'Mini community' conditioning because the only 'community' that counts in Biblical terms as far as judgment is concerned, is the community of the perfection of the Trinity, by which standard we are all equally sinners lost without hope or deliverance. We only escape from that situation if we cling by faith to the Cross of Jesus through which we can discover forgiveness, become adopted as God's Children and become objects of his Love.

This does not mean by the way that there is no right and wrong, or good and bad behaviour, not at all, God hates sin and so should we and neither does this point mean that we, as a society, as the Church and as Christians should not do our very best to promote goodness, a high morality and resist, even fight against the evil and corruptions of the world. Bad things are still bad things, evil is still evil and society needs to be protected from that which, and from those whom, inflict such evils upon us. What this does mean, however, is that the 'motivations' for resisting such things need to be those that reflect, the nature of God as revealed to us in the teachings of Jesus and the New Testament, which of course we do know is characterised most definitely by such things as Redemptive Love, Peace and Hope.

When I was a police officer I arrested thousands of people over my 30 years in the Metropolitan Police. I didn't arrest them out of a sense of revenge or because I judged them as less human than myself or even out of anger (although I will confess that some crimes make me very angry and sad because of the pain they inflict on the innocent). I arrested them in order to 'save' and 'protect' those within our society who were the vulnerable victims of their evil deeds and to promote the Redemptive Love, Hope and Peace of God within these victim's lives. In relation to those criminals that I arrested my hope was always that they would find some reformation through the Justice system and as such I felt and still feel, that in doing this, I was doing my best to reflect at least something of the nature of the 'community of God' within my work life.

We can, then, and should strive to resist evil and 'do' good works but never out of a sense of superiority, judgment and de-humanisation. This is when we go wrong as we find ourselves falling into the trap of the sort of Pharisaic self-righteousness that Jesus so readily condemned.

Perhaps one of the best examples of this sort of de-humanisation is found within the current (I assume it will still be current by the time I finish this book) debate within the Church of England around the issue of Homosexuality.

It is a fact that many Christians within the Church consider Homosexuality to be 'wrong', that is to be a style of living condemned by God and incompatible with a Christian profession. Many in fact, within this group also hold a great deal of animosity towards anyone who might disagree with this view. But why is this? And why, (as we are using this subject as our test case) does it seem that the Church is so obsessed with this particular 'so called' sexual sin?

To start with it seems interesting to me that the Church has always tended to view sexual sins (including sex outside marriage / masturbation etc) as so much worse than others. In the Bible it seems obvious that ALL sins are treated as equally in badness terms anyway. Sexual sin, for example, is placed on the same par as telling lies and various other quite 'common' and certainly 'less serious' sins, as seen in 'community' terms anyway. So why this particular obsession?

For the evangelical Christian we know that the Apostle Paul was pretty hot on the condemnation of sexual sins and was seemingly of course anti-gay (Romans 1 for example). As such his teachings can easily act (wrongfully) as a springboard for prejudice in those who might already be predisposed (by their own 'mini community' conditioning as above) to certain negative views on sexuality.

For the Anglo Catholics we have in addition to the Pauline teachings, the influence of the Roman Catholic Church with its view on, homosexuality, priestly celibacy and its historical rejection of women through male only ordination.

Put all these together and then also add the sort of conservative Victorian reformed theology on which I was brought up, together with all the other underlying emotional / psychological undertones that the Church loves to impose on us when it comes to anything to do with sex and we have femininity and sexuality in general subdued, subjugated and except in very strict circumstances i.e. within Marriage, condemned.

Now there may have been good reasons why the Apostle Paul wrote so strongly about sexual sin; his own personal character seemed to have been somewhat subdued (single but with a 'thorn in his flesh !!). He also, of course, would have been like the rest of us, conditioned by his own upbringing and 'mini community' exposure as a Jew. He also had all sorts of very unsavoury practices to deal with in his early Church congregations (love feasts at Corinth (orgies) masquerading as celebration of the last supper for example!)

There may be arguments which support the Roman Catholic Church's choice to subjugate sexuality. Regardless, these views, I would suggest, have influenced the Church and even society outside the Church. They have impacted in a highly negative way, on us as individuals and within us on a deeply subconscious level, helping to produce this prejudice and for sure there are also other more personal, sociological and psycho-sexual influences at the root of such views that together all shape our rejection of homosexuality. In the end what we find ourselves actually doing is simply submitting to a **life script** conditioned and brought into being by the influence of our own 'mini communities' which have driven us to believe that **"they are not as good as me".** We have not therefore come to this view because we really understand how God sees them but because we have been influenced by forces from outside of ourselves to judge, condemn and to see them as less human than ourselves.

To press home the point let's assume for a moment that those who are in gay relationships are sinning. I should stress that I am not here suggesting that this is my own opinion. They don't believe that they are but let's assume they're wrong. Are they by doing this any more of a sinner than you or me? Are they, if they are Christians, any less a part of Gods family? Are they, less loved, forgiven and saved by their faith in Christ than you and me? Or is homosexuality then the one sin that God left out on the Cross? Are they still my brother / sister? should I love them or treat them as outcasts? Is discrimination a correct Christian response towards other Christians or to anyone else for that matter?

Yes, we can debate the issue of homosexuality, yes, we can disagree and yes, we can seek to persuade each other of the wrongness of our views, but should we marginalise, abandon, reject even a little and dis-empower our brothers and sisters in Christ because of their sexual orientation? I don't think so. But they are living in sin I hear the conservative's cry! --- Aren't we all?

Finally, and before I finish this section I ought perhaps to attempt to answer a question which will inevitably arise in the minds of some, as a result of this debate. Does this mean, then, that we as Christians should embrace unconditionally everyone who claims to be a Christian regardless of how they live? Well, of course, I have to say no, and I say no because some styles of behaviour, damage others and by doing so cross a variety of different moral lines. In such circumstances morality often conflicts, so the moral prerogative to embrace all might have to give way for example, to one which promotes the protection of others.

So, say we have a member of the Church who is beating his wife or hurting children or a member who is bullying another, or one who is casually having sex with anyone they fancy; these behaviours we would have to challenge. But even then, we need to act without losing sight of even these perpetrators humanity and without losing sight of the fact that even despite their behaviour God still longs for them to repent; discover his grace and to be embraced as his Children.

Phew, that was a biggie too wasn't it? So, God loves us all equally that was my point. Prejudice has no place in the Church and those who practice it need to stop, step back, look at how their subconscious life scripts are defining their behaviour and learn to "love the Lord our God with all their heart, soul and strength and <u>love their neighbour as they love themselves"</u>. (That is definitely in the Bible.)

Myth 5: The inerrancy of the Bible:

Life script – 'I am more comfortable and feel safer and more secure when my life is ordered'

O my God, I can hear the chorus "stone him". Well, before you hurl the rocks just hang on a moment. The first question which we need to consider for this topic is of course 'what do I mean by the doctrine of the inerrancy of scripture? For some, in my own experience, the idea of Biblical inerrancy seems to be closely aligned with the Islamic view of the Koran, a view which is in no place reflected within scripture itself.

Many Muslims believe that the Koran is an exact copy of God's Holy writing as contained in heaven, so even when translated it ceases to be the Koran (that's why it is learnt in Arabic). It is therefore perfect in every way, every jot, full stop etc and naturally completely without error or for that matter cultural influence.

For those who also understand the idea of Biblical inerrancy in a similar way, and many seem to, the Bible assumes the characteristics of what Spiritualists would call 'Spirit - guided automatic writing'. In other words, when the disciples wrote the N/T they did so under the all-controlling influence of the Holy Spirit, as if he literally guided every stroke of the pen. As opposed to the view, I would hold, that the writing of the Bible was an inspired partnership; a product of God and man working together, neither subduing the other's creativity or influence. It is also important to note on this point that this seems to be the way that God has ALWAYS worked in relation to humanity, in creation he employs Adam and Eve to look after the world; during the flood he recruited Noah to build the ark and save his creatures; in the days of the prophet's, he used men to convey his message and guide his people and ultimately, even in Christ himself. In Christ he came into the world as a divine human being working then in a perfect partnership of humanity with the Divine to bring into the world his message of salvation! God could have done all these things differently and avoided all the pitfalls that working with humanity have clearly caused since creation, but he didn't. Working in partnership with humanity seems to be God's way of doing things. The Bible, I would suggest, is no different.

A further problem, of course, for those who hold an 'Islamic style' view of the Bible's inerrancy, is that this literalistic view of scripture is never taught in the scriptures. The one passage which alludes to how we should see the writings of the Bible states that "all scripture is inspired by the Holy Spirit" or "God Breathed" and good for the building up of the Church. The statement that it therefore contains nothing of the different writers fallen humanity and cultural influence is, I am sorry to point out, simply an assumption, an interpretation on the part of those who created this particular view. Frankly, it flies in the face of scripture itself once you actually try to understand it properly, as any student of theology will tell you, evangelical or not.

Partnership, then, seems to be God's thing with all the dangers and weaknesses that go with it. God always involves us in what he does because that is the way he chooses to act and to suggest that Scripture is any different seems just un-God-like.

Scripture is inspired, of course, but it is also the product of a partnership; a number of creative, honest, and devout men working in relationship to, and with, God by the presence of his Holy Spirit to produce a most holy collection recording God's new revelation to the world.

Is believing the Bible to be inerrant in the 'Islamic style' then a bad thing? Well, quite possibly it is because when you think about it, it makes God out to be at times rather different from that which we have seen in the revelation of Christ. For example, I led a Bible study once on the Fall of Jericho recorded in Joshua chapter 6. In this story the Lord commands the Israelite army to 'Dedicate the City to the Lord' which results in them slaughtering every living thing within the city, men, women, children and all the animals! Mass murder basically. The sort of genocide that we have all seen recently being perpetrated by terrorist groups like ISIS, in the name of their Faith. In the Bible study I dared to suggest that perhaps this was not really what God had wanted. I personally, in the light of the New Testament, cannot imagine God as one who would be too happy with the wanton slaughter of innocents; call me a sentimentalist if you like, but hey!

My suggestion was, that rather than this actually being God's will or actual command, it had been inspired in the writer's and in Israel's mind-set by the cultural view of the day in which Israel at that time had seen their God, as the other surrounding nations did, as a God of War. The proof that Yahweh was the true God was if they won in battle. The command recorded as being from God 'to go forth and slaughter the innocents' was in fact not from God at all even though the Bible said it had been. Now this didn't seem to me, anyway, to be too unreasonable a suggestion. My mistake, as a number of the Good and true stood up and harangued me off the podium as a heretic.

We should see the Bible, then, as a treasure of truth. Primarily it purports to be a Revelation (revealing) of God written by devout godly men inspired by the Holy Spirit in a partnership with God. It is a revelation containing the influence of all parties involved, a book to be understood for the wonderful thing it is without pretending that it is something that it isn't. To do that is potentially dangerous, insults its creation and lessens the real impact that it should have on our lives.

Myth 6: Perfectionism -

Script - "I will love myself when I am better"
Romans chapter 7.

[15]*I do not understand my own actions. For I do not do what I want, but I do the very thing I hate.* [16]*Now if I do what I do not want, I agree that the law is good.* [17]*But in fact it is no longer I that do it, but sin that dwells within me.* [18]*For I know that nothing good dwells within me, that is, in my flesh. I can will what is right, but I cannot do it.* [19]*For I do not do the good I want, but the evil I do not want is what I do.* [20]*Now if I do what I do not want, it is no longer I that do it, but sin that dwells within me.*

[21] *So I find it to be a law that when I want to do what is good, evil lies close at hand.* [22]*For I delight in the law of God in my inmost self,* [23]*but I see in my members another law at war with the law of my mind, making me captive to the law of sin that dwells in my members.* [24]*Wretched man that I am! Who will rescue me from this body of death?* [25]*Thanks be to God through Jesus Christ our Lord! So then, with my mind I am a slave to the law of God, but with my flesh I am a slave to the law of sin.*

2 Corinthians chapter 12.

"I was given a thorn in my flesh, a messenger of Satan, to torment me. Three times I pleaded with the Lord to take it away from me. But he said to me, "My grace is sufficient for you, for my power is made perfect in weakness." Therefore, I will boast all the more gladly about my weaknesses, so that Christ's power may rest on me. That is why, for Christ's sake, I delight in weaknesses, in insults, in hardships, in persecutions, in difficulties. For when I am weak, then I am strong."

See also, 2 Corinthians chapter 4 'Treasure in Clay Pots'

As a young Christian I was brought up to strive towards perfection, a quest that seemed to represent at that time the best response to the Bibles teaching on discipleship. For me, however, this quest rather than proving to be a positive experience led instead to a young life filled with guilt and self-recrimination as I tried, but always failed, to live in the way that I thought God expected me too.

As I got a little older however, I came to realise that I was indeed living under a completely false premise. What I would now call the 'Myth of Perfectionism', the belief that 'IN CHRIST' it might be possible, in an ideal world, to eventually live a sinless life if only one could live in a close enough relationship to God and harness enough of the power of his Spirit.

So, in this chapter I thought it might be interesting for us to consider our need, in spite of the importance of living for Christ, to accept the limitations of our ability to follow Christ. I thought that we might do this through the two passages quoted above. The first from Paul's letter to Rome where the Apostle bravely talks about the inevitable duality of our / his nature, despite being within Christ. The second from his letter to the Church at Corinth in which the Apostle talks about his own struggles with sin and about the 'thorn in his side.'

Many within the Church seem to have an image of the Apostles as the perfect men of god, and this is no doubt an image that has been fostered by the Church throughout the ages. Whilst these men have rightly become the heroes of the Church, this 'Veneration' of the Saints is something, which I find, at times a little difficult. Although to have great examples to emulate is fine, to be encouraged to aim for the impossible can, as I explained above, be a pretty frustrating and damaging experience as we simply struggle on in our often failing and comparatively pathetic Christian lives. Consequently then, Paul's admission here of his own obviously intense battle with his flesh and his equally difficult 'thorn' have become for me, a source of incredible comfort as I try but fail to live the best way I can for Christ.

Some Roman Catholic writers think that the 'thorn' denotes a lack of piety on Paul's part, an inability perhaps to be as disciplined as he could have been in some area of his spiritual life.

Martin Luther, John Calvin, and other Reformers interpreted the expression as denoting a temptation to unbelief; to a lack of Faith. Others suppose the expression refers to an actual physical pain, epileptic fits, or in general, to some other severe physical infirmity. Another view is that this "thorn" was referring to the fact that Paul had an easily aroused temper. And finally, some think that it referred to his wife!

What it exactly was, then, we just don't know but what we do know is that it was something which made Paul more like us, in as much as it made him weak. Paul struggled, Paul was far from perfect and like us this was something which Paul even as the greatest Apostle of all time, had to incorporate into his Christian life.

In what is possibly the most human of all his writings he comments on this very struggle.

Romans chapter 7

15 "I do not understand what I do. For what I want to do I do not do. But what I hate I do."

18 "I know that nothing good lives in me, that is in my sinful nature. For I have the desire to do what is good but I cannot carry it out. 19 For what I do is not the good I want to do no, the evil that I do not want to do-this I keep on doing"

And more interestingly, perhaps than this, is the fact that rather than condemn himself Paul incorporates this weakness into his life by separating his will and his motives from the weakness of his human nature.

16 "Now if I do what I do not want, I agree that the law is good. 17. as it is, it is no longer I myself that do it, but it is sin living within me."

20. Now if I do what I do not want to do, it is no longer I who do it, but it is sin living in me that does it"

Paul, then, not only embraces God's forgiveness but also forgives himself for his weakness, he even disowns it! This isn't me, he protests, I love my God, this is rather a shadow of myself, a dark passenger who lingers. This is my old self and he is dead to God crucified with Christ. In a cry of independence Paul refuses to cater for any attitudes of self-recrimination. Paul, the real Paul is free. For Christ has set him free.

And finally, Paul seeks to be rid of his thorn, he seeks perfection. 2 Corinthians 12 vs 7 - 9

7 Therefore, in order to keep me from becoming conceited, I was given a thorn in my flesh, a messenger of Satan, to torment me. 8 Three times I pleaded with the Lord to take it away from me.

But his answer is perhaps not what we might expect.

9 But he said to me, "My grace is sufficient for you, for my power is made perfect in weakness."

Definitely a bit of a surprise to the perfectionists amongst us! Not either, perhaps, the answer that Paul expected or for that matter wanted.

Doesn't God want to make us the best, the most successful Christian supermen and superwomen? On this reading perhaps not. In contrast to those who would propound the above-described perfectionist theory of discipleship, this passage points us in a different way, to a way which focuses the glory, not on our ability to always achieve, but actually on Gods ability to shine through us and to work in power through us despite our weakness's.

<u>2 Corinthians chapter 4</u>

[6] For God, who said, "Let light shine out of darkness," has shone in our hearts to givethe light of the knowledge of the glory of God in the face of Jesus Christ. [7] But we have this treasure in jars of clay, to show that the surpassing power belongs to God and not to us'

The 'thorn' then, represents, for us, our simple fallibility. It represents all our failures; the fact that we are weak. It puts to bed the sometimes-common Christian belief that God is looking for us to become perfect in this life. What we forget, in fact, is that God's power and God's Grace is best exemplified through the fact that he is willing to accept, us, love us and to work through us, even though we are a fallen humanity. The miracle of the Gospel is that despite everything we are, he is still here; that he has re-entered the world, re-entered our lives, become involved with us, in us and through us despite the fact that we all have our thorns. It is his Spirit working in all this that brings new life. Most importantly, that God can do this best, it seems, not when we are feeling supremely self confident but only when we are aware of this truth and are forced through an honest recognition of our very real limitations to rely solely on him alone. When we recognize that Gods power is made perfect not in our strength but in our weakness.

In this, as in many other things, the Gospel turns the world's priorities on its head which means indeed that Paul, for Christ's sake, can now say: *Therefore, I will boast all the more gladly about my weaknesses, so that Christ's power may rest on me. (2 Corinthians 12 vs 10)*

Paul, rather than seeking to become the 'superman', learns by this experience to allow God more access to his <u>real life;</u> to let God have more freedom within all of himself, even to allow God access to those parts of his life, which beforehand, he may have been tempted to hide from God.

In realising that he isn't, in fact, as strong as he thought he was, in accepting his weakness, sin and limitations, he falls back into a far deeper and more comprehensive spiritual surrender, which in turn allows Christ to use him and to shine through him even more than before. He then learns to incorporate his weaknesses as well as his strengths into his Christian experience.

To portray the heroes of the Church as models of perfection has been, then, a genuine mistake and the sort of Western infatuation with success that has fuelled, in places, a Gospel message bound up in an ever more intense quest for 'spiritual success' and 'prosperity' has led many down a path of Self-righteousness, over self-confidence and many others, to experience, not joy in their Christian lives but frustration, depression, guilt and self-deprivation.

This message seems then, completely in conflict with the true Gospel message of God's acceptance, forgiveness of, and love for us his children.

May God bless us sins, failures, weaknesses, thorn's and all.

Section 2 – Theology

I can't think of anymore 'Myths' that annoy me as intensely as the above so time to move on to Section two where I thought I might try my hand at some theology. Now I need to say right now that having read a number of theological books in the past mine will be nothing like them. I am just not that clever and don't have the patience to list all the different arguments from the Church Fathers to Bultmann, McQuarrie, Ladd, Cullman, Guthrie (who taught me at London Bible College: brilliant man) or of course N. T. Wright the Anglican Church's latest and greatest New Testament theologian. So, with fair warning for the avid young buck studying theology, this section will probably only annoy you to distraction.

Having of course been through my student theology days I know how much students love to debate every point ad infinitum. This I won't be doing either. My only intention in the following chapters will be to have a go at some of the basic biblical questions; ones which, I feel, we as everyday Christians, find a little hard to get a handle on. I hope that this offering brings some simple insights into 'Why we believe, what we believe.'

So here we go.

Chapter 1

The Divinity of Jesus:

In the Christian faith Jesus Christ is believed to have been both fully man and fully Divine (I'm already confused) but what is the evidence within the New Testament that has led the Church to believe in Christ's Divinity? And how can we try to understand how God may have accomplished this miracle?

Firstly: Did Jesus believe he was Divine?

Well, it seems that he did. For example, in St John's Gospel Jesus is recorded as referring to himself as the 'I AM'; a phrase that would have been instantly recognisable to any good Jew as a reflection of the quote by God to Moses at the 'old burning bush affair', you know when God calls Moses to save his people from the bad old Egyptians. Moses asks God "whom shall I say sent me?" and God say's "I AM". This was, then, one of the holiest names for God in Judaism so when Jesus says, for example, "before Abraham was I AM" he **is** claiming divinity. Then if you add all the other 'I AM' sayings to this as well, such as, 'I AM' the good shepherd or 'I AM' the bread of life, the gate for the sheep etc then you get the point.

Furthermore, Jesus also claimed on numerous occasions to have the same authority and power as God. To forgive sins for example. He also exhibited powers only reserved in Jewish thought for the action of the Divine; power over the natural elements, he calmed the storm, created food, healed the sick and of course on three occasions he raised the dead back to life. We should note that sometimes when he did these things local Jews tried to stone him for blasphemy. They certainly understood the meaning of these claims and actions. So, Jesus, we can conclude, according to the best evidence certainly believed that he was Divine.

Secondly: Did the early Church believed this? Well again yes, they did and without question. Firstly, we have passages like John's Gospel chapter one where John wrote of Jesus as the Word that became flesh. Not much doubt there about what John was saying, and although some theologians may cast doubts on who the author of John was and debate when John was written, (which raises some issues of course), John's Gospel does show, at least, that at some point early on in the life of the Early Church, the theology of Christ's divinity had been firmly established.

In addition to John's Gospel we also have the much earlier writings of the Apostle Paul and in particular the following recorded in Paul's letter to the Philippians chapter 2.

5In your relationships with one another, have the same mindset as Christ Jesus:

6Who, being in very nature [a] God, did not consider equality with God something to be used to his own advantage; 7rather, he made himself nothing by taking the very nature [b]of a servant, being made in human likeness. 8 And being found in appearance as a man, he humbled himself by becoming obedient to death— even death on a cross!

9 Therefore God exalted him to the highest place and gave him the name that is above every name, 10that at the name of Jesus every knee should bow, in heaven and on earth and under the earth, 11 and every tongue acknowledge that Jesus Christ is Lord, to the glory of God the Father.

See also, such passages as Colossians 1 vs 15-20, Hebrews 1 vs 1-4 and there are naturally other references which I am sure you can find.

However, perhaps one of the most significant pieces of evidence to support the idea that the earliest Christian Church believed that Jesus was divine is raised in an article I read years ago written by one of my old NT testament lecturers R.T. France entitled 'The worship of Jesus: A neglected factor in the Christological debate' published in the book 'Christ the Lord'. It comes not from a textual argument but from the simple and quite obvious fact that the very first and earliest Christians clearly addressed Jesus as 'Lord' (the name for God) and worshipped him! Simply read, for example, the salutations at the beginnings of Paul's letters, typically *'Grace to you and peace from God our Father and the LORD Jesus Christ'* we can clearly see then that to worship Jesus was a practice from the very earliest days of the 'Church's' existence. The early Church just naturally saw Jesus in this way. In Peters sermons in Acts we find Jesus as the 'Saviour'(4vs 12), as the 'author of life' (3vs 15 and 5:31) also as the giver of repentance and forgiveness. He is also the Judge in (10vs 42) and we likewise find this natural veneration of Jesus as Divine in the evidence from the earliest martyrs. Stephen prayed directly to Jesus at the point of his murder, as did Ananias. See Acts chapter 7 and 9 respectively. Perhaps finally, we should also note the incredibly significant fact that these very first Christians were absolute, raving monotheistic (only one God believing) Jews! To worship anything other than God then, was like a capital crime. It was something they would simply never do. To worship Jesus was an unadulterated confession that they sincerely believed that he was indeed Divine.

The early church, then, also believed that Jesus was divine and from its earliest days built, it would seem, this belief in his divinity directly from Jesus own pronouncements about himself.

The development of this understanding of Christs divinity was nevertheless an extraordinary development for these Jewish believers and cannot be explained simply from their experience of the teachings of Jesus. Something else of significant magnitude must have occurred in order for these early followers to have developed and with such sincerity, what was for them an utterly outrageous and blasphemous theology. To my mind this development could only have been finally secured through their witness and experience of two events; namely, the Resurrection of Jesus from the dead and the pouring out of God's Holy Spirit at Pentecost. Without these two events the teachings of Jesus would have died away and passed into history. Paul himself tells us that without the Resurrection our faith is a fraud. Christ's Resurrection was the act that confirmed in the first believer's hearts and minds that everything Jesus had said and done was true. In the giving of the Holy Spirit the first Christians discovered the very presence and divine power of this Risen Divine Jesus intimately within their lives.

The worship and veneration of Jesus by the earliest Christians stands tall as a testimony to the fact that they truly and sincerely experienced these two life transforming events. This, for us from the standpoint of history, should fill us with a sense of wonder, Joy, and security. They witness in a truly almighty way, the truth of our Gospel claim that Jesus was indeed divine; that he rose from the dead and that he subsequently sent his Holy Spirit upon his early Church and has continued to do so ever since in order to confirm his divine risen presence within the Church's life.

So, the church believes and has done since the beginning, Jesus was divine but how can we understand this? Well, the truth is of course, that no-one really knows my suggestion below then is simply what seems to make most sense to me.

Perhaps the best key then, to help us towards the answer to this question is found in the passage referenced above from Paul's letter to the Philippians. The Apostle Paul copies out what appears to have been one of the earliest hymns or creeds of the Church in, which Jesus is proclaimed as "being in the very nature, God." It tells us that Jesus in their view, was 'naturally Divine' and that he didn't *become* divine at some later stage after his birth. He was by his nature Divine from his very conception. My own attempt or route to understanding this most particularly difficult concept revolves around an interpretation of the 'unique nature' of the human Jesus' ***Spiritual relationship*** with God his Father and how he came to be in such a unique relationship. Somehow, it seems to me, that Jesus' ***relationship*** to God the Father was so perfect that he was, even from his conception in 'his very nature, God.'

I will try to explain;

Firstly, I just can't quite get into any theory of Jesus' divinity which appears to cut him in two, where one part was human, and another or the rest of him divine.

What we seem to be trying to comprehend, rather, is an idea where the human and divine 'aspects' of Jesus' nature were in some incredible way mixed together in order to create some sort 'blended divine human' version of a human being. I am reminded a little of the old lynx 3 deodorant advert. The one where the various pairs of gorgeous girls run headlong into each other to produce in a puff of smoke a far sexier single third model.

In my view, the key to going some way to understanding the divine nature revolves then around two things. Firstly, the indwelling of the Holy Spirit within Mary and its role in the creation of Jesus at his conception. This is of course the point behind the virgin birth story. Secondly, the development or impact of that incredibly intimate, united and all-consuming spiritual relationship within Jesus the man as he grew and became an adult. I also find this idea of the Holy Spirit's role within this process most appealing because, in a very small way, it also bears some relation to the spiritual experience of Christians ever since the birth of the Church at Pentecost.

Since the Holy Spirit was given to the Church at Pentecost, it is, has been and still is, the common experience of Christians when finding faith, to discover an ever-deepening relationship with God by the indwelling presence of his Holy Spirit. In the Bible much is made of this and in particular by the Apostle Paul who talks in a variety of ways about how this new relationship in the Spirit is meant to bring people into a closer communion with God and transform them into beings more reflective of God's character. The Spirit lives within us in order to communicate God to us and makes us more like him. Perhaps it would be consistent to suggest that this process of transformation is a small reflection of what happened within the conception and life of Jesus. God, by his Holy Spirit, indwelt Mary initiating his conception, creating a divine

/ human embryo from which there developed a perfect and all-encompassing human / divine person, existing within a perfect spiritual relationship to God the Father.

By the time he appears in our history his nature has, through the action of the Holy Spirit, become so in tune with God's nature that he could be recognised as being one who was indeed "in his very nature, God" he was then, in all that he thought, said and did, 'the very image of the invisible God'. A human being still but a human being who was also divine by nature, and as such, a perfect representation of who God is. He is divinity and humanity in a perfect partnership / relationship, the divine present and impacting on our world.

Now I realise, of course, that this concept of 'How' Jesus the man was also a divine man doesn't answer all the issues, but then again, I haven't read of any theory that can. However, this does seem to be consistent with the Church's experience of the work of the Holy Spirit. It confirms the biblical idea of the Holy Spirit as the person within the Trinity who is the 'active creator' within the God-head (God *breathed* into man and he became a living being, as in Genesis for example) and it seems to me to 'protect' the very important belief that Jesus was both human and divine in a way that doesn't diminish either 'aspect' of his nature which is fundamental to any theology of his divinity. Finally, this theory makes most sense to me.

Chapter 2

Jesus as the Son of God:

Easy this one, honest!

The phrase 'Son of God' believe it or not is really not that difficult to get a handle on. Most Christians, in my experience, actually have the basic idea already without even thinking too much about it and do so because all of us have that in built automatic understanding of what it means to be either a parent or some- one else's child.

Human sonship obviously contains two basic qualities: that of being genetically related to another person and that of being one half of what should be the closest of personal relationships. In short, the idea contains the concepts of both <u>genetic</u> and <u>relational</u> bonding.

The relationship described as being a 'Son of God', within the Bible is in fact quite similar in as much as it is also defined by these same two characteristics.

Adam, for example, is described as the Son of God just as Seth is described as the Son of Adam (Luke 3:38) simply because Adam owed his creation directly to God's intervention and because he had initially an intimate relationship to God.

Israel are described as God's firstborn (Exodus 4:22) and Christians (all over the N/T) as 'Sons of God' exactly in order to stress the same two points. Firstly, their creation by God (as a state in Israel's case through Abram and then Moses, and for Christians through their spiritual birth by the Holy Spirit) and secondly the intimacy of their <u>relationship</u> to God.

So, the concept of Biblical Sonship, <u>in general,</u> is defined by these same two ideas of a 'genetic' (well sort of genetic) / Creational link to God and on the 'personal relational' connection to God.

In the specific case of Jesus the same basic concept is used, albeit in a considerably amplified form.

Firstly, Jesus shares God's nature intimately (the Virgin birth demonstrates this point creating the Genetic / creational link) and secondly, he has, as we have described above, a unique and intimate personal / Spiritual relationship to his Father. As such then he can be called God's Son.

The uniqueness of Christ's sonship (And we all know that he is uniquely different of course) is bestowed on or attributed to Jesus in Biblical terms because of his **role** within God's plan. That is, because of his designation as the Messiah /Saviour. Jesus rather than being **a** Son of God then, i.e. one among many, becomes **THE** (one and only unique) Son of God because he is the one sent who firstly, uniquely shares in the Fathers nature and who secondly **comes to DO his Fathers will in the salvation of his people.** This is of course witnessed right at the beginning of our Gospel story at Jesus' Baptism at which point Jesus first accepts and is commissioned for his Ministry and then again at his Transfiguration. At his Baptism God is heard to say; 'This is my Son whom I love, with him I am well pleased'. At the Ascension 'This is my Son whom I love, with him I am well pleased, listen to him'

Sonship, for Jesus then, contains this added theological concept of **mission and obedience** which sets him apart biblically from everyone else.

In conclusion, the biblical concept of Jesus as **the 'Son of God'** contains these three characteristics; the creational, the relational and his obedience to the unique role he had to play as God the Father's Messiah. These three together made Jesus biblically, **THE Son of God.** (See told you it was easy, didn't I!)

Chapter 3

Jesus: The Messiah.

As we touched on this description of Jesus, above, I thought we might have a go at this one next. As with the Son of God title most Christians seem to have a fairly good grasp of this one too.

The term Messiah or Christ is without doubt one of the most important N/T descriptions of Jesus and encompasses both 'who' Jesus was and 'what' he came to do.

In the O/T perhaps the most important reference to the coming Messiah (particularly as the term came to be understood in later Judaism and at the time of Jesus) is found in Isaiah chapters 9 and 11 where '*the one to come*' is described in the following terms, he will, "smite the earth with the rod of his mouth, and with the breath of his lips he will slay the wicked" (he is as you can see something of a supernatural figure). "He will purge the earth of wickedness, gather faithful Israel together and reign forever from the throne of David over a transformed earth!"

Sounds a bit grim really doesn't it, but this was the typical picture that Israel developed of their salvation and you can understand why, after all they were always in the poo in some way or another, either condemned by the prophets, conquered by another country, enslaved or bullied. Even in the time of Jesus they were a conquered nation under the rule of Rome. One can forgive them, then, for thinking that evil ruled the world and that they needed a supernaturally led deliverance from their God to put things back into the right order. Being a sort of, let's say, rather optimistic bunch they figured that the end result of this onslaught on evil and recreation of the world by God, through their Messiah, would be their dominance as a nation over all the world under the rule of this super Messiah in the name of their God! (Never had small dreams these Hebrews did they?)

Needless to say, then, by the time Jesus burst onto the scene this hope of the final Messianic deliverance was at its peak. For Israel this had become the typical view of what would happen when their Messiah finally arrived. He would be Israel's supernatural, conquering King.

We see this expectation and hope most obviously described biblically in the preaching of John the Baptist.

Matthew 3:7-11 New International Version (NIV)

> *7 But when he saw many of the Pharisees and Sadducees coming to where he was baptizing, he said to them: "You brood of vipers! Who warned you to flee from the coming wrath? 8 Produce fruit in keeping with repentance. 9 And do not think you can say to yourselves, 'We have Abraham as our father.' I tell you that out of these stones God can raise up children for Abraham. 10 The axe is already at the root of the trees, and every tree that does not produce good fruit will be cut down and thrown into the fire. 11 "I baptize you with water for repentance. But after me comes one who is more powerful than I, whose sandals I am not worthy to carry. He will baptize you with the Holy Spirit and fire.*

John the Baptist, clearly, also expected Jesus to be this supernatural conquering King bringing both the wrath of God on the evils of the world and the all-consuming 'Fires of Judgment'.

The problem with this, however, both for John and in particular for the Jewish leaders of his day was that Jesus just didn't see his mission as Messiah in these more popular armed revolutionary terms at all. His mission, as he saw it, turned out to be something very different, namely, to bring God's Kingdom rule into the world of course, but in a completely different way, that is, to bring it within our hearts and through the transforming personal experience of the Holy Spirit. This Hebrew vision of a violent political mission was actually never a part of his agenda, which is why of course most Israelites rejected his claims.

That Jesus did advertise his Messianic identity however is found in a number of ways.

Firstly:

The main mission of the Messiah was believed to be the re-introduction of the Kingdom of God (that is the rule or authority, presence and power of God) into the life of Israel and this Jesus claimed to do in almost everything he did. He interpreted, for example, his miracles in this way and in particular his acts of deliverance. He also claimed to have defeated Satan and to be "plundering his house".

Jesus and Beelzebul Mathew 12 vs 22-29

22 Then they brought him a demon-possessed man who was blind and mute, and Jesus healed him, so that he could both talk and see. 23 All the people were astonished and said, "Could this be the Son of David?"

24 But when the Pharisees heard this, they said, "It is only by Beelzebul, the prince of demons, that this fellow drives out demons."

25 Jesus knew their thoughts and said to them, "Every kingdom divided against itself will be ruined, and every city or household divided against itself will not stand. 26 If Satan drives out Satan, he is divided against himself. How then can his kingdom stand? 27 And if I drive out demons by Beelzebul, by whom do your people drive them out? So then, they will be your judges. 28 But if it is by the Spirit of God that I drive out demons, then the kingdom of God has come upon you.

29 "Or again, how can anyone enter a strong man's house and carry off his possessions unless he first ties up the strong man? Then he can plunder his house.

The whole 'temptations experience' was, in fact, about just this point. That through his resistance Jesus defeated Satan and because of this was able to start bringing God's Kingdom into the lives of all. Jesus also claimed to forgive sins, another Kingdom benefit, and if you look you will see that the list of, otherwise divine prerogatives, goes on.

Specifically, however, Jesus affirms his Messianic position when he confronts his disciples in Mark chapter 8 (also Matthew chapter 18) when he asks his disciples "who do people say I am?" Peter, as we know, replies "You are the Christ (same meaning as Messiah) the Son of the living God" Jesus replies "Blessed are you Simon Bar-Jona! For flesh and blood have not revealed this to you but my Father in heaven" -pretty plain.

Finally, Jesus raised the dead! He rode into Jerusalem on Palm Sunday in a clear fulfilment of the most commonly (at that time) recognised Messianic prophecy contained in the book of Zechariah chapter 9 and in the end this proclamation was the reason he was executed. He told the Sanhedrin that he would 'sit at the right hand of God' the Messiahs place, and when asked by Pilate, refused to deny it. So, all the Biblical evidence suggest that Jesus clearly believed he was the Messiah.

But what did he mean by this?

As we have already said, in Israel at the time of Jesus, the most commonly held belief regarding the role of the Messiah was that he would bring to an end the rule of evil and usher in the Kingdom of God. He, God's anointed, would wage a sort of Holy war from which Israel, with him as their righteous King, would rise victorious and rule the nations. Through him Israel would be gathered up and brought back to their rightful place on a 'renewed world stage' and this obviously involved a hugely political agenda including, naturally, the defeat of Rome along with all that was corrupt.

Was this also the concept of Messiahship that Jesus adhered to? Well obviously, not.

Jesus did, of course, see himself as the Messiah and in almost everything he did he demonstrated his belief that through him the Kingdom rule of God was re-entering the arena of mankind. Where Jesus differed from the popular view, however, was 'HOW' the new Kingdom was entering the world; HOW it was influencing the lives of mankind and WHEN this longed-for recreation of the universe would occur. Now this is a huge subject but, as always, I will try to explain it as simply as I can.

Chapter 4

The Kingdom

Right from the very start of his ministry Jesus attempted to re-evaluate Israel's traditionally held, rather confrontational view, of the Kingdom. For example, in the Sermon on the Mount he encouraged his followers to love their enemies, pray for those who persecuted them and for them to be peace makers. Rather than seek to stir up insurgency and unrest, he counselled unity.

For Jesus, the kingdom was not coming in by the sword (as the Jews had expected) but by the power of God's own forgiveness and love. The Kingdom was seen not so much as the conquering of a physical or geographical place but as the influencing by God of people's hearts.

The term the 'Kingdom of God' then refers not so much to a 'place' or to the 'conquered new land' but to a *situation.* The kingdom exists where God's rule, presence, power, and authority become present. So in present terms when we become a Christian and allow God to become involved directly within our lives; when he comes to live intimately with us by his Spirit's presence; when we give God the authority over our lives, when we become his subjects by our own choice we step 'into', become a member of, his kingdom and receive with that by our decision of faith, all the benefits that go with it, namely, adoption as God's children, forgiveness, an experience of the Holy Spirit, eternal life etc. In N/T terms, then, the Church universal is where God lives, moves and exerts his kingship. Therefore, the Church (in all its 'forms') is the place where the Kingdom exists on earth. Get it?

For Jesus, then, the Kingdom begins to re-enter into the lives of men and women as they come into contact with and come to accept his new revealing of God. As they allow him and his ministry to influence their lives, they enter into the rule of God i.e. they enter into his kingdom.

For Jesus, then, he is bringing back God's Kingdom but not by way of violent revolution but by way of leading people back to a new type of communion with God.

And his work continued after Pentecost (and continues today) through the work of the Holy Spirit through the ministry of the Church.

Further to this, we read in Jesus' teachings, that the Kingdom is going to grow, like a mustard seed which grows into a huge tree or like a piece of yeast in some dough. The kingdom's influence, whilst tiny at first i.e. in his limited ministry, will become more influential drawing membership from all over the world. This is the meaning behind the 'Parables of growth' they are prophecies fulfilled after Pentecost and ever since as the Church has grown over the last 2000 years.

What will be the end result?

The end result of this re-emergence of the Kingdom of God will in fact be in some ways very similar to the original Jewish hope, in the end God will act to destroy all evil and recreate the universe at the Armageddon. One day then, the kingdoms influence will come to a climax and a conclusion, one day all tears, pain, evil and corruption will be done away with and be replaced by the perfect new order, where the resurrected saints will live with Jesus, Gods Messiah, as their eternal King. OK?

The characteristics and benefits of the kingdom:

Now that the new kingdom of God is here and active, we ought to look a little at what this means for the believer.

These are the basic characteristics which define the kingdom's presence. The presence of the Rule of God as king, a new relationship and communion with God by the presence of his Holy Spirit, and the growth of a new Spirit-filled community (the Church) in which these two aspects find their expression and through which this new rule of God comes to influence the world God created. The Kingdom, then, becomes the place where God is acknowledged in Christ, through Christ and by faith in Christ, to be King.

The benefits of joining this kingdom through Faith in God's appointed Messiah are basically a new relationship with God, forgiveness and eternal life. We will deal with these next.

The new relationship:

To his first disciples Jesus was a great teacher, a prophet, a revolutionary and a miracle worker. Charisma must have flowed out of every pore of his body but none of these aspects of their relationship to him was, I believe, the one that intrigued them the most. None of these were the reason they stayed, followed and eventually died in his service. By far the most appealing aspect of their experience with Jesus, I believe, must have been the incredible intimacy with the divine that they felt when in his presence, Jesus himself described this aspect as being like "Spirit and life" to his disciples. When they were with him they felt they were in the presence of God. It was this aspect of their relationship with Jesus that they so missed after his crucifixion. Jesus warned them not to worry promising 'another comforter', the 2nd Paraclete, but when he was gone and the 'presence' gone with him they fell apart, only to be revived at Pentecost when the Spirit came to re-initiate the connection.

The 'new' relationship with God, then, was what set their experience of Jesus apart from anything they had ever known before. To put it most simply that is exactly what we should be experiencing today as members of God's Kingdom principally, because of the formerly mentioned Spirit giving event we call Pentecost.

The whole purpose of the Spirit's coming was not then, as Pentecostalism would teach, to give the disciples a 'second blessing' and the gift of speaking in spiritual tongues. The purpose of Pentecost was, as it states in the passage, to fulfil the prophecy contained in the Old Testament book of Joel where God had promised Israel that one day he would come back to them and initiate a completely new type of relationship with his people; *"I will write my laws in their hearts, all will know me from the greatest to the least".* Pentecost was the event which initiated the new possibility of intimate communion with the divine. The Spirit came to Christ's new Church and gave it its birth as the place where God now lives, moves, and has his being. Since Pentecost it is this aspect which defines the Church and which makes it completely unique. As Christians we join this Church by becoming a part of this new experience initiated by our own spiritual new birth at our conversion to faith in Christ.

So, we 'know' God; we experience him by his Spirit's presence and through this we receive everything which characterises the new kingdom. The N/T describes this situation of communion with God in various ways; for example we are 'Born Again', 'sons (and daughters) of God', we are a 'New Creation', we are 'the body of Christ' and so on. All, however, in basic terms are different ways of describing the significance of our new situation as people who now live within this new and unique communion / relationship with God.

Chapter 5

Forgiveness

Now, God's forgiveness is a tricky thing to really grasp. It sounds as if it shouldn't be, but for most of us it is and tricky because, frankly, we are not used to experiencing it. After all, most people that I have met don't really forgive at all. Some don't forgive because it's not their nature and prefer revenge as satisfaction. Others don't because they can't, usually because they are too hurt. Some try to forgive, some don't care about forgiving, and some just 'need' to be angry because it is this that sustains them. If you live long enough, all of us, I suspect, will at some time perhaps share all these experiences. I know I have.

The simple fact is that we are not that used to experiencing the type of forgiveness that God offers and as a result, find it hard to understand and accept.

The quality of forgiveness God offers us in Christ is unique, you see, because it is absolutely complete and (in my opinion) not at all linked to the history of our lives. I'll explain what I am trying to say.

The most basic of Christian beliefs is that when Jesus died on the Cross, he took upon himself all the sin of the world, yes? That is, he 'paid' the price due to the world for its sin and corruption.

God was angry and filled with wrath and Jesus absorbed all that anger onto himself. The punishment he suffered acted as a vicarious sacrifice, he died in our place. The result of this act was that God's wrath and judgement was completely satisfied (done, gone, finito, you get the idea) and because of this God can bestow upon mankind, through Christ, his complete forgiveness and we as individuals can appropriate this gift now if we accept the rule of his Messiah (Saviour) by Faith. OK?

Because this forgiveness is complete, it follows logically that it cannot contain any element of personal history. It stems, if you like from the end of time. God has seen ALL the sins we will ever commit and has provided a forgiveness which covers them all NOW. So, forgiveness becomes what theologians call, an 'Eschatological blessing'. It contains all the elements of that which will exist in the forgiveness of God's END TIME kingdom. (we talked about that above). We can't ever, once we have become truly a member of the new kingdom, become 'not' forgiven, and our standing in God's sight cannot change if we sin tomorrow or next year or in ten years etc.

This also means, by the way, that God will never see us as anything other than a holy person. He will not be angry with us again; he will not walk away from us, hide from us or cut himself off from us (all of which I have heard some Christians suggest). WE ARE, NOW, BECAUSE OF JESUS, OBJECTS ONLY OF HIS LOVE and it is the miracle of this situation which makes everything else possible.

Why then, if we have already received forgiveness for the whole of our lives, even that part of our lives we have yet to experience and live through, do we still need to ask for forgiveness?

The immediate question which comes from that is why are we supposed to ask for forgiveness, as we are encouraged to do in the Lord's prayer? Many assume that because of this the above position is somehow wrong, but how can it be? If there are no more sacrificial offerings needed for sin (a fact which the Apostle Paul clearly states) then why should prayers of repentance, which is an offering after all, be *necessary?*

The reason, I would suggest, we are encouraged to live a penitent life is tied up in the fact that we are in a relationship with God which involves not God's need to feel right with us but does involve our need to feel right with Him. Just as with anyone else whom we love, if we do wrong to them then *WE* need to feel that we have put it right. It is also, of course, important *FOR US* to re-connect with the truth of God's forgiveness. It is also, of course, the right thing to do, a natural part of our nature, and if nothing else, at the very least polite. What it definitely isn't is *THE MEANS* by which we acquire more forgiveness.

Why not just keep on sinning and not worry about it? Well, we just shouldn't want to! At the end of the day if we have truly discovered the incredible grace of God in our lives and have experienced his presence and the depth of his Love for us then, as with any other loving relationship, we should want to do the best we can to live in a way that we believe pleases God. Makes sense doesn't it?

The point is that God isn't blackmailing us or holding us to ransom. We don't live in the fear that if we fail, God will reject us. Our failure is already built into the equation, '*who WE are cannot act as a condition to who God is or how He treats us*'. We are clean before God because that is how he CHOOSES to see us. All we can do is try and choose to do the best we can in response to such amazing grace.

Paul explains this whole suggestion most clearly in Romans chapter 6.
Romans chapter 6

Dead to Sin, Alive in Christ

6 What shall we say, then? Shall we go on sinning so that grace may increase? [2]By no means! We are those who have died to sin; how can we live in it any longer? [3]Or don't you know that all of us who were baptized into Christ Jesus were baptized into his death? [4]We were therefore buried with him through baptism into death in order that, just as Christ was raised from the dead through the glory of the Father, we too may live a new life.

[5]For if we have been united with him in a death like his, we will certainly also be united with him in a resurrection like his. [6]For we know that our old self was crucified with him so that the body ruled by sin might be done away with, [a]that we should no longer be slaves to sin— [7]because anyone who has died has been set free from sin.

[8]Now if we died with Christ, we believe that we will also live with him. [9]For we know that since Christ was raised from the dead, he cannot die again; death no longer has mastery over him. [10]The death he died, he died to sin once for all; but the life he lives, he lives to God.

[11]In the same way, count yourselves dead to sin but alive to God in Christ Jesus. [12]Therefore do not let sin reign in your mortal body so that you obey its evil desires. [13]Do not offer any part of yourself to sin as an instrument of wickedness, but rather offer yourselves to God as those who have been brought from death to life; and offer every part of yourself to him as an instrument of righteousness. [14]For sin shall no longer be your master, because you are not under the law, but under grace.

Slaves to Righteousness

[15]What then? Shall we sin because we are not under the law but under grace? By no means! [16]Don't you know that when you offer yourselves to someone as obedient slaves, you are slaves of the one you obey—whether you are slaves to sin, which leads to death, or to obedience, which leads to righteousness? [17]But thanks be to God that, though you used to be slaves to sin, you have come to obey from your heart the pattern of teaching that has now claimed your

allegiance. *¹⁸You have been set free from sin and have become slaves to righteousness.*

¹⁹I am using an example from everyday life because of your human limitations. Just as you used to offer yourselves as slaves to impurity and to ever-increasing wickedness, so now offer yourselves as slaves to righteousness leading to holiness. ²⁰When you were slaves to sin, you were free from the control of righteousness. ²¹What benefit did you reap at that time from the things you are now ashamed of? Those things result in death! ²²But now that you have been set free from sin and have become slaves of God, the benefit you reap leads to holiness, and the result is eternal life. ²³For the wages of sin is death, but the gift of God is eternal life in Christ Jesus our Lord.

OK?

Chapter 6

Who will be saved?
Hell, and Judgement?

Just a small subject this one

What is Hell? Is there really such a place? Who is destined to go there? Now, these are easy questions for the traditional conservative evangelical.

"Hell, is a place of torment where all those who haven't accepted Christ in this life go forever, after they die; it exists (some-where) and is a place of torment and is eternal."

The problem, of course, for those who don't like this idea (including me) is that on the face of it, it seems to accord well with some of the teachings of the New testament. For example, Jesus spoke of a place where the corrupt would go after death, a place of 'weeping and gnashing of teeth' and Jesus also mentions the apparent damnation of the un-believers in parables such as the sheep and the goats!

However, a closer look at some of these teachings can, if we are open minded demonstrate perhaps a slightly more complicated scenario.

To begin with, in the New Testament, the word used to describe the location of God's final judgment is 'Gehenna' which is assumed of course by many, to be the name of an Eternal and Spiritual destination. However, this designation has a broader meaning. It is originally in fact, a reference to a place called the 'Gehinnom' valley, which is to this day situated just south of Jerusalem.

It appears that historically it was the place where sacrifices and even child sacrifices were offered to the heathen God Molok. This is recorded in such passages as 2 Kings 16:3 and 21:6 there are also references to acts of divination and sorcery. These practices were subject to the condemnation of Jeremiah who called for these shrines to be destroyed.

Jeremiah 7:31-34

31They have built the high places of Topheth in the Valley of Ben Hinnom to burn their sons and daughters in the fire—something I did not command, nor did it enter my mind. 32So beware, the days are coming, declares the LORD, when people will no longer call it Topheth or the Valley of Ben Hinnom, but the Valley of Slaughter, for they will bury the dead in Topheth until there is no more room. 33Then the carcasses of this people will become food for the birds and the wild animals, and there will be no one to frighten them away. 34I will bring an end to the sounds of joy and gladness and to the voices of bride and bridegroom in the towns of Judah and the streets of Jerusalem, for the land will become desolate.

Their destruction to prevent Child sacrifices is recorded in **2 Kings 23:10.**

10He desecrated Topheth, which was in the Valley of Ben Hinnom, so no one could use it to sacrifice their son or daughter in the fire to Molek.

Furthermore, we find that the valley only became equated with the hell of the last judgment after Jeremiah uttered threats of Judgment over it.
Jeremiah 19

19 This is what the LORD says: "Go and buy a clay jar from a potter. Take along some of the elders of the people and of the priests 2and go out to the Valley of Ben Hinnom, near the entrance of the Potsherd Gate. There proclaim the words I tell you, 3and say, 'Hear the word of the LORD, you kings of Judah and people of Jerusalem. This is what the LORD Almighty, the God of Israel, says: Listen! I am going to bring a disaster on this place that will make the ears of everyone who hears of it tingle. 4For they have forsaken me and made this a place of foreign gods; they have burned incense in it to gods that neither they nor their ancestors nor the kings of Judah ever knew, and they have filled this place with the blood of the innocent. 5They have built the high places of Baal to burn their children in the fire as offerings to Baal—something I did not command or mention, nor did it enter my mind. 6So beware, the days are coming, declares the LORD, when people will no longer call this place Topheth or the Valley of Ben Hinnom, but the Valley of Slaughter.

⁷"'In this place I will ruin [a] the plans of Judah and Jerusalem. I will make them fall by the sword before their enemies, at the hands of those who want to kill them, and I will give their carcasses as food to the birds and the wild animals. ⁸I will devastate this city and make it an object of horror and scorn; all who pass by will be appalled and will scoff because of all its wounds. ⁹ I will make them eat the flesh of their sons and daughters, and they will eat one another's flesh because their enemies will press the siege so hard against them to destroy them.'

¹⁰ "Then break the jar while those who go with you are watching, ¹¹and say to them, 'This is what the LORD Almighty says: I will smash this nation and this city just as this potter's jar is smashed and cannot be repaired. They will bury the dead in Topheth until there is no more room. ¹²This is what I will do to this place and to those who live here, declares the LORD. I will make this city like Topheth. ¹³The houses in Jerusalem and those of the kings of Judah will be defiled like this place, Topheth—all the houses where they burned incense on the roofs to all the starry hosts and poured out drink offerings to other gods.'"

¹⁴Jeremiah then returned from Topheth, where the LORD had sent him to prophesy, and stood in the court of the LORD's temple and said to all the people, ¹⁵"This is what the LORD Almighty, the God of Israel, says: 'Listen! I am going to bring on this city and all the villages around it every disaster I pronounced against them, because they were stiff-necked and would not listen to my words.'"

It could be argued, then, that the idea of Hell itself as referenced to in the NT was an idea created from a physical place which then developed, over history within Judaism, to become that which we see referenced in the Gospels and New Testament.

Jesus 'use' of the idea of 'Gehenna'

In the New Testament it is important to note that references to 'Gehenna' are used, in the most part, by Jesus as a means to encourage / persuade / even frighten people into living a pure and Christian life. For example:

- Matthew 5:22: " *But anyone who say's 'you fool' will be in danger of the fire of hell.*" (Gehenna)

- Matthew 5:29: "*If you right eye causes you to sin gouge it out and throe it away it is better for you to lose one part of your body than for your whole body to be thrown into hell*" (Gehenna)

- Matthew 5:30: "*and if your right hand causes you to sin cut it off and throw it away. It is better for you to lose one part of your body than for your whole body to go into hell*" (Gehenna)

- Matthew 10:28: "*Do not be afraid of those who kill the body but cannot kill the soul, rather, be afraid of the one who can destroy both body and soul in hell*" (Gehenna)

- Matthew 18:6 – 9 "*If anyone causes one of these little ones—those who believe in me—to stumble, it would be better for them to have a large millstone hung around their neck and to be drowned in the depths of the sea. 7Woe to the world because of the things that cause people to stumble! Such things must come, but woe to the person through whom they come! 8If your hand or your foot causes you to stumble, cut it off and throw it away. It is better for you to enter life maimed or crippled than to have two hands or two feet and be thrown into eternal fire. 9And if your eye causes you to stumble, gouge it out and throw it away. It is better for you to enter life with one eye than to have two eyes and be thrown into the fire of hell. (Gehenna)*

- Matthew 23:15: "*Woe to you, teachers of the law and Pharisees, you hypocrites! You travel over land and sea to win a single convert, and when you have succeeded, you make them twice as much a child of hell (Gehenna) as you are.*

- Matthew 23:33, to the Pharisees: "*You snakes! You brood of vipers. How will you escape being condemned to hell*" *(*Gehenna)

- Mark 9:43: "*It is better for you to enter life maimed than with two hands and go into hell* (Gehenna) *where the fire never goes out*"

- Mark 9:45: "*And if your foot causes you to sin then cut it off it is better for you to enter life crippled than to have two feet and be thrown into hell*" (Gehenna)

- Luke 12:4-5 "*I tell you, my friends, do not be afraid of those who kill the body and after that can do no more. 5But I will show you whom you should fear: Fear him who, after your body has been killed, has authority to throw you into hell.* (Gehenna) *Yes, I tell you, fear him."*

We should also note that these passages are directed at the already converted! Even at the disciples themselves! They are clearly filled with hyperbolic language, *language which no-one actually believed or believes was meant to be taken literally.* No-one hearing Jesus statements here, for example, would ever have thought that he really meant for them or us to start cutting off our limbs or gouging out our eyes in order to ensure our holiness *and there is certainly no record of any of the disciples of Jesus doing this.* The message that Jesus seems to be primarily conveying within these texts seems to have far more to do with persuading the disciples of the importance of preserving the quality of one's holiness, commitment and faith, and much less to do with predictions regarding destination Hell!

Within this same context Jesus says to his followers, '*do not lose your saltiness for once lost you cannot become salty again!* I believe this is impossible! This is primarily and clearly, then, a command to preserve and persevere in order to sustain their effectiveness within the future ministry of the Kingdom.

In Matthew 10:28-42 the whole context of the passage is intended to persuade the disciples not to reject their faith in the face of coming persecution. Jesus tells them '*do not fear those who can kill the body but not the soul, rather be afraid of the one who can destroy both body and Soul in Hell'.* Jesus gives here, then, his disciples a stark warning of the negative and divisive effects that his Kingdom message will have on families and within the community in which they live. This is not at all surprising considering these first disciples and their communities were Jewish. The threats of Judgement described are set out, then, to specifically dissuade the disciples from consciously rejecting his Gospel message in the face of such persecution and trauma. In short, this whole passage seems to be Jesus' way of, and in the strongest possible terms, persuading his disciples not to forsake the cause. Rather than a passage which seeks to set out a program describing those who will go to heaven or hell. " *Anyone who loves his Father or Mother, Son or daughter more than me is not worthy of me, and anyone who does not take up his cross and follow me is not worthy of me, Whoever finds his life will lose it and whoever loses his life for my sake will find it"*

All these passages above then *could* be read as Jesus employing hyperbolic language (over exaggerated language not meant to be taken literally) in order to persuade his disciples to persevere in holiness, faith and in their commitment to the new ministry of the Kingdom.

I can remember my less than politically correct grandmother telling me that "if you don't eat the crusts your hair will go curly!" or "if you're not good the bogy man will get you". There was of course no way that failing to eat the crusts of bread would make my hair curly and clearly there was no bogey man either, that was not the point. The point was to make us eat our crusts or go to bed on time!

In the parable of the sheep and the goats, which is Jesus' most comprehensive treatment of the idea of judgment, Hell is described as a furnace of fire for the 'Devil and all his angels.' This seems to me to be an important distinction which we will come back to shortly.

Matthew 25:41 New International Version (NIV)

41 "Then he will say to those on his left, 'Depart from me, you who are cursed, into the eternal fire prepared for the devil and his angels".

Within other Gospel passages we find that the 'fire and torment' aspects are missing altogether, and that the final punishment is pictured more in terms of separation from God. It is ***outer darkness,*** for example in Matthew chapter 8:12; 22:13; 25:30 and as ***exclusion from the presence of Christ*** in Matthew 7:23 and in Chapter 25:12!

It is true that Jesus did refer at times to the concept of judgment. He claimed to be the eschatological (end time) Judge before the Sanhedrin and made 'casual' references to the day of judgement in Matthew 10:15, 11:22, 24, 12: 36,41,43 and 23:33. He also mentions the 'separation of men' in one passage (Matthew 13:41, 49). However, it is important to note in this passage, the Parable of the weeds, that the weeds are again referred to as the ***'Sons of the devil'*** and that at the end of days Christ's angels will weed out all that ***'causes'*** sin and all who ***'do evil'.*** This I feel, as already stated is an important distinction.

The only place where Jesus is recorded as dealing extensively with the question of Judgement is in The Parable of the Sheep and the Goats (Matthew chapter 25) but even within Matthew 25 the idea that this is a depiction of a hell, where individuals go to be punished, is thrown off course. As many a theologian has pointed out in this passage Jesus is describing the judgment of 'the nations'. The focus, then, in this passage is on 'community' or 'national judgment'. Furthermore, the basis of Gods future judgment is described as *how* the accused have collectively treated Jesus' disciples rather than on how any *individuals have responded* to the call to Faith!

Even if we were to take wider interpretation of the text, we cannot escape the difficulty that the Judgment described is based on whether or not people have acted with kindness and charity! Faith doesn't seem to be within the equation at all, which of course also raises some significant complications when trying to understand this as a description of 'destination hell' based on a refusal to accept faith in Jesus.

In summary then, it seems fair to say to the open-minded thinker that, the picture so far is at least *more complicated* than the rather simplistic interpretation of hell/judgement stated by some who hold the most conservative of positions.

So where do we go from here?

Perhaps it might be good to start with what we appear to know for certain:

Firstly, we know that when Jesus came to earth, he re-introduced through his ministry, the presence of the kingdom.

Secondly, we know that whilst on earth entry into the kingdom was defined by virtue of an acceptance of him and his message by faith.

Thirdly, we know that when Jesus died, he carried upon himself the sins of the whole world throughout time.

Fourthly, we know that there will be a time of judgement where the nations of the world (and by extension, individuals) will face Christ. We know that he, will, by his sacrifice, be the 'means' by which anyone gets to become a part of the fulfilled Kingdom of God (i.e. gets into heaven). We also know that as the Christ / Risen Messiah, he will also be the one who inaugurates and manages the whole process of God's judgment.

Finally, we know that he has been given all power and authority in these matters and that he will reign as the king of a newly formed and perfect universe in which the resurrected humanity will live in harmony forever.

We may also, <u>reasonably suggest</u> from the evidence (even despite the points made above) that there may well be a situation, or place 'outside' of this 'end time' Kingdom, where 'those who are described as '***the Devil and all his angels****'* will exist in separation from any sense of this divine grace. This place we may postulate to be a place of suffering but to be fair one must accept that little information exists as to exactly what the ***nature*** of this place might be and the information that does exist is somewhat inconsistent.

'Who' and Why?

Who goes where and why? Well, this is, of course, the crux of the issue and for me, taking the picture as a whole, it seems fair to conclude a few things:

Firstly, it seems pretty clear to me that the key to finding salvation **in this life** within the N/T is entry into the kingdom of God and that for Jesus and the N/T writers the 'means' by which people enter into the new kingdom in this life is by faith in Christ.

However, this by no means answers the following questions:

- What happens to those who don't come to faith in Christ in this life?

- What happens to those who sincerely worship God through other faiths?

and finally:

- If the key to not getting into the Kingdom is a <u>conscious rejection</u> of the Gospel message, (which many on the evidence do) then what happens to those who never get a realistic chance to understand and accept the Gospel in this life? Furthermore, what constitutes a realistic chance?

The suggestion that all these millions of souls end up 'automatically' and simply by default within some sort of hell is surely, in the end, only a 'reverse assumption' based on limited evidence at best. Perhaps, even more importantly, is an enormous 'comment' on how we really see the nature of the God, who according to the New Testament is apparently the perfect expression of Love!

Is it then possible that God may have further plans for those outside the Church of Christ on Earth that Jesus either wasn't aware of or at least was never commanded by God the Father to reveal? Can we really say with certainty that what we have in our Gospel records is EVERYTHING of God's plan for humanity?

A few thoughts to consider on this point:

1. Why, if only those relatively few who are lucky enough to receive the 'complete' opportunity to respond to the Gospel are going to be saved, did Jesus die for the sins of the **whole world and for all time?** (Bit of an over-kill if you will excuse the pun)

2. Jesus **_did_** die for the sins of the whole world and for all time. This, I assume, is a given within all mainstream Christian thought. Apart from some more extreme Calvinists who seem to believe that Jesus only died for the elect! (see above)

3. If judgement is based on a 'rejection' of the Gospel, then 'when' have people really had the chance? And what qualifies as a complete hearing and understanding the Gospel?

4. When are individuals to be considered by God as being *evil* and fall into the category Jesus describes as '*the Devil and all his angels*'?

5. To expand on the comment above, if God's character is described within the New Testament as being perfect love, frankly, doesn't that quality in itself suggest that within God's decisions there must be also the perfect elements of justice, fair play, compassion and inclusion? Can we really conceive of a God who loves his humanity so completely, sending the vast majority of his creation to a place where they will suffer in pain and torment for all eternity?

A final suggestion: 'The limited knowledge of Jesus.'

In a number of passages within our Gospels we find Jesus expressing not only his intimacy with the Father but also his <u>distinctiveness from the Father</u> and never more so than in the Gospel of John where there is, in addition to this emphasis, a further element which some theologians describe as a theology of the *'limited knowledge' and 'subservience' of the human Jesus to his Father in Heaven'*. This idea is expressed within John's Gospel in a number of ways; for example: Jesus has been sent by the Father. He is described as one who obeys the Father's commands: I John 15 vs 10. In John chapter 5 vs 19-20 Jesus can apparently do nothing of his own accord. In John 14 vs 10,24 and in Chapter 17 vs 8 his words are the Father's, and the Father is greater than the Son! Finally, in Mathew chapter 24 Jesus openly confesses that even he has no idea when the Father will usher in the 'end of days'!

The Day and Hour Unknown - Matthew 24.

The Day and Hour Unknown

[36] *"But about that day or hour no one knows, not even the angels in heaven, nor the Son,* [1] *but only the Father.* [37]*As it was in the days of Noah, so it will be at the coming of the Son of Man.* [38]*For in the days before the flood, people were eating and drinking, marrying and giving in marriage, up to the day Noah entered the ark;* [39]*and they knew nothing about what would happen until the flood came and took them all away. That is how it will be at the coming of the Son of Man.* [40]*Two men will be in the field; one will be taken and the other left.* [41]*Two women will be grinding with a hand mill; one will be taken and the other left.*

[42] "Therefore keep watch, because you do not know on what day your Lord will come. [43] But understand this: If the owner of the house had known at what time of night the thief was coming, he would have kept watch and would not have let his house be broken into. [44] So you also must be ready, because the Son of Man will come at an hour when you do not expect him.

What we have here then is a human Jesus who is subservient to God, sent by God in some way having less authority than God and most importantly with a limited knowledge of God's final plan for the end of the universe! Interesting hey!

We are not saying here that Jesus wasn't the image of the invisible God or that everything that 'he was' wasn't perfectly divine. But what we *are saying* is that Jesus wasn't *ALL THAT GOD IS*; we are saying that his divinity was pure but that he was *limited,* and this surely seems obvious from the evidence.

It appears, then, that Jesus while he was on earth, didn't know everything that God the Father knew! As such it seems fair to hope that perhaps his Kingdom message was, and is not, after all the *whole story* of how God will deal with the universe at the end of days! I am *absolutely certain* by the way, that *our own* interpretation of that message is definitely not the whole story.

My own belief is that the simplistic theology of Judgment and Hell that some more conservative evangelicals would like to propose is by no means as clear within the New Testament as they would like us to believe. My own hope is that God has far more in store for the humanity of this world than our Gospel reveals, more grace and a greater plan for the salvation of mankind.

We have a Gospel to preach. We must preach it faithfully and, whatever happens, believe that 'the Christ of God's love' Jesus, will be at the centre of all that does come. But that doesn't mean that we can assume one single interpretation of 'the end of days' or make predictions as to the reality and content of an Eternal Hell or assume that anyone who does not fit into 'our box' will go there. Surely God's capacity to Love and save is greater than our capacity to judge and decide!

Chapter 7

The problem of Evil.

After having worked as a serving Police Officer in the London Metropolitan Police for 30 years I have become increasingly convinced in the reality of evil within our world. I am quite convinced that I have experienced it's presence on numerous occasions. I have also, I believe, experienced the presence of evil within the context of my Christian ministry as a Priest. I therefore do not personally have any issue with the idea of the existence of evil its presence and influence within our lives, within society or for that matter its influence within the Spiritual lives of believers within the Church.

The big questions for me are: firstly, what is Evil, that is, how should we define it? Secondly, from where does it come?

The answer to these questions is by no means a simple one. For example, evil is described in some cases as simply the 'absence of good'. In others, in terms of a 'destructive morality' or as 'actions which cause harm to others' the roots of which find their 'basis' within such human motivations as anger, jealousy, rage, suffering, selfishness, hatred, psychological illness and the like.

In religious terms, evil, in addition to this, is often described as the presence or influence of a spiritual force outside of humanity, which corrupts humanity influencing people to carry out *'the evil that we do'.* This is generally speaking the view of most Christians to one extent or the other.

These questions of definition and genesis also raise issues of consistency, cause, and responsibility. Is it really possible, for example, to consistently define the meaning of 'good or bad, right or wrong'? Can morality be universally agreed or is it relative to culture and the accepted norms of any particular society or group? If it is, which seems to be an inescapable fact, then how can we truly know if something *is* right or wrong? As I have argued earlier on in this book we all have to accept, regardless of whatever definition or decision we make on these issues, that all of us without exception have already been conditioned to believe in 'what we choose to believe' by the 'communities' within which we have existed since birth. Those communities could be our family, our school, our friends, our society, or our Church. This explains, also, why our moralities differ even within any single society or group like the Church community for example. There is, then, and will always be to some extent or another a diversity of morality within any community and within the world. The best hope we can have towards achieving a wholesome and constructive morality, (that is, to be able to 'correctly' define what IS actually good or bad, right or wrong) is to hope that the communities in which we have lived and do currently live are communities that have promoted and communicated the most constructive loving and positive moral standards into our lives so far. We are all products of where we have been, where we are and of those by whom we have been influenced.

This also raises issues in relation to the second question addressing the 'nature and origin' of 'the evil that some do' and to the questions of 'ownership and responsibility'. For example, it is commonly believed that those who have suffered from abuse are also more likely to become abusers themselves; that children who have grown up in an emotionally damaging environment will exhibit destructive and aggressive behaviour; that damaged people in general terms damage others. In some cultures, marrying and having sex with children under 16 is perfectly acceptable, whereas in Western society it is illegal!

As a serving Police officer, I arrested and prosecuted huge numbers of criminals most of whom essentially saw nothing expressly wrong with the crimes they had committed. They were convinced, as a result of their circumstances and upbringing that what they were doing was justifiable for one reason or another and morally acceptable because of this. This would be the case even for those who committed the most heinous of crimes, crimes like rape, paedophilia and even murder!

On one occasion, whilst working in North West London my colleagues and I attended a call to a domestic disturbance. On arrival at the property, we found the lady of the household in her kitchen calmly drinking a cup of tea. On enquiring if she was O.K. she replied "Yes, fine thanks, he's in the bedroom, he's dead, I stabbed him to death with a kitchen knife". Sure enough there was the husband lying on the double bed, dead as a dodo, with a large kitchen knife sticking out of his Chest. It transpired that for a number of years he had been beating his wife and finally she had had enough. So, when he came home drunk that evening, she had waited till he fell asleep on the bed and then, with no sense of conscience or regret, stabbed him to death. Now, I can hear many of you already saying, 'well he got what he deserved'. But she could have just had him arrested and / or left him or taken some other course of action prior to Murder, she didn't and felt perfectly O.K. about the situation because her circumstances had conditioned her to quite 'happily' commit the crime and to see murder, wrongly but understandably perhaps, as justified and her only viable option. In other case's I have seen paedophiles who 'easily' justify their crimes along with burglars, robbers and rapists.

Many of these people would be, in my understanding at least, carrying out acts which I would define as evil as 'anti God'. The difficult questions are: why are they doing this? Where does this propensity for evil come from? How do we set the standard by which we attempt to successfully judge what is acceptable and what is evil? If we are all products of what our experiences have made us, or indeed if the influence to do evil comes, at least in part, from a spiritual force outside ourselves then, what moral guidelines or basis do we use in order to hold people accountable for the evil that they do?

Within the Penal system of the United Kingdom these issues are addressed in number of ways:

Firstly: there is a national standard of acceptable behaviour, namely, the Law, which in this country, thankfully, is based on Christian Biblical precepts.

Secondly: again, thankfully, as a result of this, U.K. society in general has a well thought out and fairly consistent moral code based on the majority of society's acceptance of the Law. Deep down we all really know that to steal, for example, is unacceptable to most of society and therefore wrong.

Thirdly: within our penal system the emphasis is on rehabilitation rather than primarily on punishment. This reflects the acceptance of the belief above, that we are all, including criminals, to some extent, products of our circumstance and upbringing. Therefore 'blame' for criminal behaviour, although not removed from the offender completely, is recognised as not to be focused entirely on the offender.

There is then, within the U.K. penal system, a very real degree of what we as Christians might call grace and understanding. The aim of our penal system is to bring reformation, healing, and repentance. Our system is judged on how successful it is in preventing offenders continuing in their acts of evil post-conviction. It is this generally Christian moral structure which makes it 'comfortable' for Christians to also be Police officers. At least that was very much the case for me throughout my whole service.

Where, however, in my opinion the current system fails society and therefore fails in its 'battle' against the 'evil that we do' is in its lack of consideration of the danger that evil (whatever its genesis or cause) poses to its victims. In the quest to recognise the human 'corporate' responsibility for criminal behaviour, that is, for evil, and in the over presumption of and desire for the possibility of reformation, the system allows 'the evil that people do' far too much freedom and access to society. As a result, this causes tremendous and preventable harm to it's citizens. There are too numerous cases to list which demonstrate clearly how many victims of terrible crimes have become victims simply because offenders were released without having, in any way, achieved any real reformation. The consequences of this lack of judgment are frankly too horrendous to quantify: houses burgled, people robbed in the street, women raped, innocents defiled and murdered. All this is because the moral prerogative of protecting the innocent and vulnerable has been overwhelmed by the desire to 'share' the responsibility for evil, by the belief that reformation of the offender should be society's **Primary** concern and by the belief that such reformation can be achieved through minimal penal, financial and psychological investment. Furthermore, of course, the system fails to give any due consideration to the possibility that there could be an outside and malignant spiritual force at work within people's lives which drives them into committing acts which we would describe as evil and which of course secular society's systems have no means or power to influence.

It seems to me that however we understand the meaning of evil or whatever we feel may be the roots of the evil that humanity does, we have a genuine problem to discuss and one which needs an answer. Evil impacts on all of us in one way or another and on some in the most horrendous ways both as victims and as those who become 'possessed' or 'influenced' by it.

It may be helpful at this stage before we try to look into evil from a biblical perspective to have a go at defining what we believe evil might be from our thoughts so far. Initially I would define evil as more than simply the absence of Good. Evil deserves, in my view, a more pro-active definition.

Evil, then, in my experience consists of *actions and behaviour which cause or inflict significant harm or distress to another human being, society, or community.* Evil itself, *__at this stage of our discussion__* cannot be separated from the 'acts' which it produces. Acts of evil committed have their genesis in the damaged emotional, mental and psychological states of those who commit them. This damage will have been caused by the 'evil-doers' previous experiences of suffering, neglect, pain, trauma and by the more subtle and perhaps less specific effects of their damaged or inadequate treatment as a child and young adult.

We may extend this definition and classify 'acts of evil' further as *any behaviour (not necessarily criminal) which contradicts or defiles the 'humanity' of another.* This naturally widens the scope of what we might consider to be 'acts of evil' considerably.

Acts of Evil from a Biblical perspective.

Biblically speaking we may also describe 'Acts of Evil' as actions which would be considered to be 'anti God' or likewise in opposition to the morality of the ethics of the kingdom of God. Which of course embraces all of the above.

The Apostle Paul certainly takes such a view.

Galatians chapter 5

[16] So I say, walk by the Spirit, and you will not gratify the desires of the flesh. [17] For the flesh desires what is contrary to the Spirit, and the Spirit what is contrary to the flesh. They are in conflict with each other, so that you are not to do whatever you want. [18] But if you are led by the Spirit, you are not under the law. [19] The acts of the flesh are obvious: sexual immorality, impurity and debauchery; [20] idolatry and witchcraft; hatred, discord, jealousy, fits of rage, selfish ambition, dissensions, factions [21] and envy; drunkenness, orgies, and the like. I warn you, as I did before, that those who live like this will not inherit the kingdom of God.

[22] But the fruit of the Spirit is love, joy, peace, forbearance, kindness, goodness, faithfulness, [23] gentleness and self-control. Against such things there is no law. [24] Those who belong to Christ Jesus have crucified the flesh with its passions and desires. [25] Since we live by the Spirit, let us keep in step with the Spirit. [26] Let us not become conceited, provoking and envying each other.

Romans Chapter 1

God's Wrath Against Sinful Humanity

[18] The wrath of God is being revealed from heaven against all the godlessness and wickedness of people, who suppress the truth by their wickedness, [19] since what may be known about God is plain to them, because God has made it plain to them. [20] For since the creation of the world God's invisible qualities—his

eternal power and divine nature—have been clearly seen, being understood from what has been made, so that people are without excuse.

[21] For although they knew God, they neither glorified him as God nor gave thanks to him, but their thinking became futile and their foolish hearts were darkened. [22]Although they claimed to be wise, they became fools [23]and exchanged the glory of the immortal God for images made to look like a mortal human being and birds and animals and reptiles.

[24] Therefore God gave them over in the sinful desires of their hearts to sexual impurity for the degrading of their bodies with one another. [25]They exchanged the truth about God for a lie, and worshiped and served created things rather than the Creator—who is forever praised. Amen...

[28] Furthermore, just as they did not think it worthwhile to retain the knowledge of God, so God gave them over to a depraved mind, so that they do what ought not to be done. [29] They have become filled with every kind of wickedness, evil, greed and depravity. They are full of envy, murder, strife, deceit and malice. They are gossips, [30]slanderers, God-haters, insolent, arrogant and boastful; they invent ways of doing evil; they disobey their parents; [31] they have no understanding, no fidelity, no love, no mercy. [32]Although they know God's righteous decree that those who do such things deserve death, they not only continue to do these very things but also approve of those who practice them.

It is quite clear then, from these and other similar passages that 'acts of evil' can be defined, biblically speaking as acts which contradict the morality and nature of God. They result within the experience of humanity, in Biblical terms, essentially because of humanity's fundamental rejection of and consequent separation from God himself.

This rejection and separation has led directly to the corruption of humanity on the most basic of levels by something that here, the Apostle calls 'The Flesh' but which can be more aptly described as the corruption of humanity's very nature by the power of sin. This is of course what the story of the Fall of Adam is meant to convey. Because of humanity's rejection of God, it has become utterly corrupted by a malevolent power (sin) and pre-conditioned because of that corruption to be by nature 'anti God' or 'evil'! No-one is exempt!

The continual quest of the moral human endeavour is to create systems and paradigms that contradict this pre-condition to evil and prevent individuals and societies from descending into chaos and self-destruction. We may also of course quite rightly from a religious perspective see within the moral endeavours of humanity the power of God drawing us back to himself through his gracious continued presence within the world; the power of his new kingdoms influence in Christ and the power of the Holy Spirit still at work within our world. All of which act as a counterbalance to the power of sin that we have so foolishly allowed to enter into God's original creation.

It is absolutely no surprise to me that when we look at the constructs and attempts by humanity throughout the ages and currently today to counteract humanity's 'sinfulness' that organisations of faith whether Christian or not have been and are always at the forefront of humanities attempts to bring a greater morality into our world. It is clear that despite our rejection of him God has never given up on us.

It is also of interest to note that in many cases, as the rejection of religion has increased so have the acts of evil that we do! Nazi Germany during World War 2 would be the most obvious example of this, although there are many others.

So far, then, we have considered the definition of Evil and considered in the main its human roots. We have also now, however, introduced the idea of the corrupting power of sin into the equation which, of course, adds a further fundamentally religious dynamic into the discussion.

Sin

In Classic Christian thought 'sin' is described as an act which is contrary to God's laws and to his nature. St Augustine of Hippo, for example, described sin as "a word or deed, or a desire which is in opposition to the eternal law of God". For Christian scholars such behaviour can be viewed as either 'a breaking of the law' or, in terms of our relationship with God, as a lack of love for God for example and the promotion of our own 'self-love' in its place. Sin is seen fundamentally in terms of actions, thoughts or desires held or committed by human beings.

Sin as a disease.

In Genesis 1 we are told that when Adam sinned 'sin entered the world' that 'sin' then corrupted everything within the created order. Adam and Eve become afraid of God, they become aware of their own vulnerability and nakedness and they become distrustful of each other. Even the very earth itself is damaged.

Genesis 3:8-22

8 Then the man and his wife heard the sound of the LORD *God as he was walking in the garden in the cool of the day, and they hid from the* LORD *God among the trees of the garden. 9 But the* LORD *God called to the man, "Where are you?" 10 He answered, "I heard you in the garden, and I was afraid because I was naked; so I hid." 11 And he said, "Who told you that you were naked? Have you eaten from the tree that I commanded you not to eat from?" 12 The man said, "The woman you put here with me—she gave me some fruit from the tree, and I ate it." 13 Then the* LORD *God said to the woman, "What is this you have done?" The woman said, "The serpent deceived me, and I ate." 14 So the* LORD *God said to the serpent, "Because you have done this, "Cursed are you above all livestock and all wild animals! You will crawl on your belly and you will eat dust all the days of your life. 15 And I will put enmity between you and the woman, and between your offspring [d] and hers; he will crush [h] your head, and you will strike his heel." 16 To the woman he said, "I will make your pains in childbearing very severe; with painful labour you will give birth to children. Your desire will be for your husband, and he will rule over you." 17 To Adam he said, "Because you listened to your wife and ate fruit from the tree about which I commanded you, 'You must not eat from it,' "Cursed is the ground because of you; through painful toil you will eat food from it all the days of your life. 18 It will produce thorns and thistles for you, and you will eat the plants of the field. 19 By the sweat of your brow you will eat your food until you return to the ground, since from it you were taken; for dust you are and to dust you will return." 20 Adam named his wife Eve because she would become the mother of all the living. 21 The* LORD *God made garments of skin for Adam and his wife and clothed them. 22 And the* LORD *God said, "The man has now become like one of us, knowing good and evil. He must not be allowed to reach out his hand and take also from the tree of life and eat and live forever."*

Clearly the 'picture' of 'sin' here is of something powerful, something apart from humanity, something that seems to have a corrupting influence on everything within the created order, rather than 'sin' being defined as 'simply' action by humankind. It has a powerful life of its own. The best analogy that I can come up with, which seems to reflect this image, is that of the virus which comes and infects everything it touches.

The Depravity of Humanity and Original Sin.

This sense of complete and total corruption, in turn, brought about within Christian thought the idea of what Christian theologians call 'Original Sin'.

Within the theology of original sin, sin is seen as a 'condition' or as a 'corruption', rather than being defined solely as an action which comes about because of the selfishness or self-obsession of humankind. It takes on more of this 'infectious' characteristic.

Sin is something which has infected and pervaded humanity, corrupting the human condition to its very core. In Christian thought the effects have been described in some cases as an inherent 'slight self-deficiency'. In other cases, as a 'human tendency towards immorality' and in the most extreme case as the 'total depravity' of humankind which in turn, leads to humankinds automatic guilt and collective guilt before God.

St Augustine, for example, followed this view basing his teaching on such passages as Romans chapter 5 vs 12-21, 1 Corinthians Chapter 15 vs 21 -22 and from the Old Testament passages like Psalm 15 vs 5,19 -23. You may well find it slightly surprising that I also tend towards this idea of our 'total depravity' but sadly it seems to reflect very well my experience of humanity throughout my life. If I consider the 30 years I spent as a serving Police Officer; the news reports that fill our T.V. screens every single day, the general experience of humanity within my own Christian and private life it seems clear to me that all of us to one extent or another have a preference to indulge in 'sinful' behaviour. Now please don't misunderstand me. I am by no means someone who has lost faith in humanity. I recognise deeply, that alongside all the selfishness, pride and evil that we demonstrate as humanity, there are also many people who manage to overcome this propensity to some extent or another. Those who fill our world with lights of kindness, selflessness, love, joy, courage and fortitude. In every community within which I have ever lived, worked or served there have been people who have accomplished this and who still do. I hope very much that I am also personally one such person. I have spent my life in the service of others either as a Police Officer or as a Priest. I have spent all of my life trying to bring peace, healing, comfort and hope to my fellow human beings. If I am to be perfectly honest, however, even within my character and after 40 years of being a committed Christian I find the battle between my own 'sinful self-interest' and my desire and commitment to be 'good' has never completely gone way. I still believe that despite all I have done for my fellow human beings and all that I still desire to do, my sinful nature crouches at the door of my life waiting to pounce! I refuse to believe that this is not a characteristic shared, if we are honest, by all of us however good we may be.

I would also ask any parent whether they have ever had to teach their children, however young, to be 'bad'? In my experience, as a parent of a wonderful 29-year-old son and two equally wonderful 5 and 4-year-old girls, the constant struggle is to show them, by example, through love and kindness how to be 'good'. 'self-interest' and 'naughtiness' seem to me, to be all children's _natural default setting_. Both my wife and I know already that our daughters are a mixed bag and that both are in constant need of direction, encouragement and love in order that they may '**become good human adults**'.

Our 'battle' then as human beings, as parents, as communities and as society does indeed seem to be a battle against our own propensity to 'Sin'. This propensity, if we are honest, seems to emanate from the very core of our nature reflecting the Genesis picture stated above.

The 'old and new natures' within the New Testament.

In the New Testament this concept of our 'battle' for goodness is clearly represented in the teachings of St Paul in his discussion of the tension between our 'old nature' which is seen as corrupt and the 'new nature within us' which has been brought about by the indwelling of the Holy Spirit through faith in Jesus. Paul clearly links this whole concept to the fall.

Romans chapter 6 vs 5 - 7

5 For if we have been united with him in a death like his, we will certainly also be united with him in a resurrection like his. 6For we know that our old self was crucified with him so that the body ruled by sin might be done away with, [a]that we should no longer be slaves to sin—because anyone who has died has been set free from sin"

Ephesians Chapter 2 vs 2 -9

Made Alive in Christ

2 As for you, you were dead in your transgressions and sins, 2in which you used to live when you followed the ways of this world and of the ruler of the kingdom of the air, the spirit who is now at work in those who are disobedient. 3All of us also lived among them at one time, gratifying the cravings of our flesh [a] and following its desires and thoughts. Like the rest, we were by nature deserving of wrath. ⁴But because of his great love for us, God, who is rich in mercy, ⁵ made us alive with Christ even when we were dead in transgressions—it is by grace you have been saved. ⁶And God raised us up with Christ and seated us with him in the heavenly realms in Christ Jesus, ⁷in order that in the coming ages he might show the incomparable riches of his grace, expressed in his kindness to us in Christ Jesus. ⁸ For it is by grace you have been saved, through faith—and this is not from yourselves, it is the gift of God— ⁹not by works, so that no one can boast. ¹⁰ For we are God's handiwork, created in Christ Jesus to do good works, which God prepared in advance for us to do.

Ephesians Chapter 4 vs 22

²² *You were taught, with regard to your former way of life, to put off your old self, which is being corrupted by its deceitful desires; ²³to be made new in the attitude of your minds; ²⁴and to put on the new self, created to be like God in true righteousness and holiness.*

Colossians Chapter 3 vs 9 – 11

⁹ *'Do not lie to each other, since you have taken off your old self with its practices ¹⁰and have put on the new self, which is being renewed in knowledge in the image of its Creator. ¹¹Here there is no Gentile or Jew, circumcised or uncircumcised, barbarian, Scythian, slave or free, but Christ is all, and is in all'.*

The reception of the Holy Spirit, then, through faith in Jesus introduces into our 'nature' a new and reformative 'power' or dynamic namely, the power of the Holy Spirit after which, we become engaged in an inner 'spiritual battle' between the old nature, which owes its 'genesis' within humanity to the corruption of Sin caused by Adam's fall and our new nature which owes its 'Genesis' within us by the indwelling of God's Holy Spirit. Again, 'sin' is identified not as 'inanimate' simply as the 'things that we do, feel or desire, but as a powerful force or virus which has contaminated us to our very core. As the Spirit indwells us now, so the force of 'sin' indwelt us first!

In our discussion, then, on the meaning of evil we find now that the 'evil that we do' we do because of the presence of a powerful 'force' or 'corruption' that has infected our humanity at its core. This drives us towards committing acts of evil within our lives, within our communities and within the world, on both a personal and corporate level.

Is there more? Thus far, then, we have decided that evil consist of actions that we do which are anti the nature and law of God and which damage the humanity, rights, peace, comfort, security, wellbeing, of other human beings. We have also suggested that the root of such behaviour lies in the fundamental corruption of the original God given human nature caused by the decision of humanity to betray God. This led to the introduction into our human nature and the created order of a powerful and corrupting force, infection, which the Bible calls Sin.

The Architect of Evil.

We now ask whether there is an 'architect' of this situation, a single figure, a malevolent being who stands as the ultimate anti God or evil influence and who has managed since the creation of the universe to orchestrate the destruction of all that God originally created and whose malevolent presence and power still pervades our existence continually seeking to manipulate and damage God's creation. This is, of course, naturally a uniquely religious question.

In my own experience both as a Christian Police Officer and a Priest it seems quite clear that any and all of humanity's own secular paradigms, structures and techniques despite the obvious and laudable effects they have on our personalities, communities and world seem, to a significant degree, to be incapable of dealing effectively with the problem of the 'human condition' that is, with the propensity, within our personalities, communities and world to contain the 'Evil that we do'. The penal system fails, the psychologist and psychotherapists fail, governments and lawmakers fail, community consciousness of right and wrong fails.

As a police officer my colleagues and I were always very conscious that the best we could do for society, despite our greatest efforts, was to 'hold back the darkness of human nature'. Our aim was always to try our best to keep the 'evil that we do' in check! We never expected to prevent crime completely, or rid the community of evil, it was here to stay. We just tried our best to keep it under some form of control!

In the medical field it is clearly apparent that the techniques for dealing with those with violent and destructive personalities are 'managed' in the same way. People with 'broken' personalities are, in the vast majority of cases, controlled by drugs rather than cured.

Within the recent corona virus epidemic rational pleas and community pressure fell on such deaf ears that laws had to be introduced to control the selfishness of those who chose to ignore the rules around social distancing.

I am not saying here that some do not learn by their mistakes, or do not get reformed by the penal system, or do not find relief through the medical systems or do not heed the power of the majority community consciousness, that would be inaccurate and unfair. Regardless of this, however, I am quite convinced that all of these successes simply add up to the same 'holding back the dark' management, that we succeeded in, to some extent as police officers.

The truth is that none of these systems or structures manage to effect any *fundamental* change in the *nature* of those they impact on. They are effective because they put in place barriers and disincentives that convince the population that to do good is more beneficial than to do harm or conversely that to do harm will simply 'cost' us too much. Likewise, on a more positive note, they create incentives which persuade us that doing good can bring us more benefit than doing bad.

In essence the majority of us live *'good'* lives because.

1. We have been lucky enough to have been conditioned to do so by our communities from childhood.

2. Because we believe that being good brings higher rewards than being bad.

3. Because we are afraid of getting caught and punished.

It goes almost without saying that we should be grateful to all those involved in providing these incentives which prevent us, our communities and our world from plunging into the inevitable chaos that would exist if these structures were not in place. Nevertheless, it is just a fact that despite thousands of years of social, legal, governmental, and medical influence the 'evil that we do' seems to carry on. The people, structures, and paradigms simply 'hold back the dark' that lives within us all. Just watch the news every day!

This inability then, of all the worlds efforts to deal with evil leads me, as a Christian, to the question we are attempting to address here.

We accept, from a Christian perspective, that there is an inbuilt infection within the human condition which we have called 'sin' against which we all battle. Is there also then an Architect of our situation who not only orchestrated the original infection but who also continues to influence humanity towards the 'evil that we do' and against whom secular humanity has no power?

This idea of an 'architect of evil' is common within many religious belief systems. We will deal with this belief as held within the Christian tradition.

The Devil or Satan.

In the Christian tradition the figure of this 'Architect' is the Devil or Satan. He is described as a 'Fallen Angel' who rebelled against God and was cast out of heaven to walk the earth. He is the antithesis of truth. He terrorizes the world and shall be condemned at the end of time judgment, together with the 'angels' that follow him. The biblical witness to his reality is clear.

Revelation 12 vs 7-10

[7] Then war broke out in heaven. Michael and his angels fought against the dragon, and the dragon and his angels fought back. [8]But he was not strong enough, and they lost their place in heaven. [9]The great dragon was hurled down—that ancient serpent called the devil, or Satan, who leads the whole world astray. He was hurled to the earth, and his angels with him.

In addition to this, within the Biblical narrative, the Devil is identified as the architect of the fall of man, the serpent who tempted Adam and Eve. Revelation Chapter 20 vs 2. *'He seized the dragon, that ancient serpent, who is the devil, or Satan, and bound him for a thousand years.'*

He is the Dragon who leads the world astray in Revelation Chapter 12 vs 9.

'The great dragon was hurled down--that ancient serpent called the devil, or Satan, who leads the whole world astray. He was hurled to the earth, and his angels with him.'

He is the prince of this world in the Gospel of John Chapter 12 vs 31 and 14 vs 30.

'Now is the time for judgment on this world; now the prince of this world will be driven out.'

'I will not say much more to you, for the prince of this world is coming. He has no hold over me,'

He is the spirit who works in the Children of disobedience in Paul's letter to the Ephesians chapter 2 vs 2.

'in which you used to live when you followed the ways of this world and of the ruler of the kingdom of the air, the spirit who is now at work in those who are disobedient.'

He is the God of this world in Pauls second letter to the Corinthians Chapter 4 vs 4. 'The god of this age has blinded the minds of unbelievers, so that they cannot see the light of the gospel that displays the glory of Christ, who is the image of God.'

He is the Tempter of Jesus in Mathew Chapter 4 vs 1.

'Then Jesus was led by the Spirit into the wilderness to be tempted by the devil.'

Jesus and the Devil

In perhaps his most significant treatment of the devil Jesus equates his victory over the devil at his temptations directly to his ability to carry out his new Kingdom ministry.

Jesus and Beelzebul Matthew Chapter 12.

22 Then they brought him a demon-possessed man who was blind and mute, and Jesus healed him, so that he could both talk and see. 23All the people were astonished and said, "Could this be the Son of David?"

24 But when the Pharisees heard this, they said, "It is only by Beelzebul, the prince of demons, that this fellow drives out demons."

25 Jesus knew their thoughts and said to them, "Every kingdom divided against itself will be ruined, and every city or household divided against itself will not stand. 26 If Satan drives out Satan, he is divided against himself. How then can his kingdom stand? 27And if I drive out demons by Beelzebul, by whom do your people drive them out? So then, they will be your judges. 28 But if it is by the Spirit of God that I drive out demons, then the kingdom of God has come upon you.

29 "Or again, how can anyone enter a strong man's house and carry off his possessions unless he first ties up the strong man? Then he can plunder his house.

Clearly within this passage Jesus makes several points.

Firstly, he acknowledges the presence of a man possessed by Demons.

Secondly, that the author of this possession is Satan or the Devil.

Thirdly, that the Devil has his own kingdom.

and finally, and perhaps most importantly, that the Devil's 'house' or 'kingdom' has been invaded by Christ. He has been 'Bound up' and rendered powerless against the presence and power of Jesus's own new ministry of the kingdom of God.

In this passage we see that not only does Jesus believe in the devil but that at sometime prior to this encounter Jesus had defeated him. This has resulted in Jesus ability to bring into people lives (Satan's property) the redeeming, liberating power of his Kingdom. It is clear on this timeline that this victory occurred as a result of Jesus' resistance to Satan during the temptations.

The issue for those Christians and Theologians who do not wish to believe in the presence of this 'living architect' this one personality who instigated, designed and continues to play a part in the 'evil that we do' seems to be simply that Jesus clearly did! For Jesus, the one divine Son of God, Satan, the Devil is a real and powerful character whose aim is to continue to corrupt and destroy the quality of our human existence as he seeks to possess our souls. As the Apostle Peter reminds us, he roams the earth looking for those whom he can devour.

1 Peter Chapter 5 vs 8

Be alert and of sober mind. Your enemy the devil prowls around like a roaring lion looking for someone to devour. 9 Resist him, standing firm in the faith, because you know that the family of believers throughout the world is undergoing the same kind of sufferings.

Conclusion

In conclusion, then, evil consist of actions that we do which are anti the nature and law of God and which damage the humanity, rights, peace, comfort, security, wellbeing, of other human beings. The root of such behaviour lies in the fundamental corruption of the original God given human nature caused by the decision of humanity to betray God. This led to the introduction into human nature (and the created order) of a powerful and corrupting force, infection, which the Bible calls sin. Finally, we maintain that the ultimate 'Architect' of this corruption, in Biblical terms, is the Devil, a Fallen Angel, whose malevolent presence continues to poison and corrupt humanity. He is active. He is real.

We take supreme comfort however in the knowledge that he is also and already a defeated enemy whose power base has been successfully infiltrated and overcome by the victory of our Messiah. He has conquered the power of sin and death through his victory at the Temptations, his life of ministry, his death and Resurrection.

Through faith in him we, as Christians, are able to step out of the dominance of Satan's power over us, resist the power of Sin and find redemption, reformation and new Spiritual life through the power of the new Kingdom of God within us by the presence of God's Holy Spirit now given to the Church. We live in a place of victory.

Chapter 8

Eternal Life.

The question of eternal life is naturally central to the faith of the Christian Church. Ultimately, we hope, that when we die physically 'who we are' will in some way continue beyond that experience. This part of us may be described as, 'the essential part of our identity' or 'as our stream of consciousness' or as, in most religious thought, our 'Soul or Spirit'. Death is our inevitable 'final and unknown Journey' and for many of us it is something that we approach with ever deepening hesitation and even fear.

Personally, I have always been extremely apprehensive about having to die. I can vividly remember at the age of five or six telling my father (a confirmed atheist) one evening as he was putting me to bed that I was scared of dying. His reply was 'well David you're not afraid of going to sleep, are you? to which I said 'no,' 'then there we are' he replied.

At the time I remember being somewhat comforted by this rather atheistic reply but in later adolescence I began to experience what I can only best describe as 'deeply terrifying panic attacks' centred the possibility of my annihilation, of my existence simply and completely ending at my death, these panic attacks would come upon me almost without warning and send me into a very 'empty' place. The depth of these panic attacks is difficult to describe. They would thankfully pass quickly but leave me deeply disturbed. They continued well into my early adult life and well after a became a Christian.

On reflection I now put these experiences down directly to this rather inadequate and 'un-hopeful' explanation about death given to me at what was a very impressionable age. This explanation had imprinted into my subconsciousness this idea of my eventual annihilation.

Eternal life, then, is something that I very much hope will turn out to be a part of my own experience when I take my final breath, as it were, on this earth.

The suggestion of a 'continuing of being' after death is common among many religions, philosophies and spiritualistic disciplines and may firstly, quite possibly be evidenced in the various and numerous experiences that so many of us have of the 'supernatural' spiritual world. In addition to the innumerable accounts evidenced by the many writers, I have known numerous people whom I trust implicitly, who are in no way psychologically disturbed or in any way prone to fantasy or mental instability who will testify at having experienced first-hand, incidents which can only seem to be explained as being 'other' than those we normally experience in the natural world. For example, some very dear friends of mine lived with what they would call a ghost or poltergeist for years. In one quite regular manifestation of its presence the husband would hear his wife calling him from the kitchen or bedroom while he was alone in the house. He would also see images flash across his vision and damp patches that would appear and then disappear on the floor of their home. These occurrences happened over such a long period of time (years) that the family became quite accustomed to these manifestations and the 'presence' indicated by them.

On one occasion their daughter's boyfriend then in his mid-20's challenged the family as to the reality of their 'ghost', they in turn challenged him to stay in the house on his own. He accepted and whilst alone in the house heard their daughter calling his name! in his words he 'freaked out'.

A number of years later, at a time when these occurrences had become more frequent, I performed a 'house blessing with Holy communion' ritual in their house aimed at sending the 'presence' away. They haven't experienced it since.

My wife had a ghostly visitor for years after her Father and brother died, he appeared as a sort of ghostly figure at night and would even sometimes lovingly tuck her into bed.

These and similar stories are far from unusual. For a couple of years after we moved into our current Vicarage and only during the days leading up to the Christian feast of 'All Souls' we experienced odd events in the house, most notably the heating thermostat being turned higher in the evenings on its own!

Quite what these incidents reveal is of course impossible to say but they are certainly common enough not to be dismissed as delusions.

In the Old testament there are also occasional references to the dead returning to instruct or guide the living. Saul and Samuels Ghost is one example below.

1 Samuel 28

Saul Talks with Samuel's Ghost

⁷ *Saul then said to his attendants, "Find me a woman who is a medium, so I may go and inquire of her."*

"There is one in Endor," they said.

⁸ *So Saul disguised himself, putting on other clothes, and at night he and two men went to the woman. "Consult a spirit for me," he said, "and bring up for me the one I name."*

⁹ *But the woman said to him, "Surely you know what Saul has done. He has cut off the mediums and spiritists from the land. Why have you set a trap for my life to bring about my death?"*

¹⁰ *Saul swore to her by the LORD, "As surely as the LORD lives, you will not be punished for this."*

¹¹ *Then the woman asked, "Whom shall I bring up for you?"*

"Bring up Samuel," he said.

¹² *When the woman saw Samuel, she cried out at the top of her voice and said to Saul, "Why have you deceived me? You are Saul!"*

¹³ *The king said to her, "Don't be afraid. What do you see?"*

The woman said, "I see a ghostly figure[a] coming up out of the earth."

¹⁴ *"What does he look like?" he asked.*

"An old man wearing a robe is coming up," she said.

Then Saul knew it was Samuel, and he bowed down and prostrated himself with his face to the ground.

¹⁵ *Samuel said to Saul, "Why have you disturbed me by bringing me up?"*

"I am in great distress," Saul said. "The Philistines are fighting against me, and God has departed from me. He no longer answers me, either by prophets or by dreams. So I have called on you to tell me what to do."

¹⁶ *Samuel said, "Why do you consult me, now that the LORD has departed from you and become your enemy? ¹⁷ The LORD has done what he predicted through*

me. The LORD has torn the kingdom out of your hands and given it to one of your neighbors—to David. [18]Because you did not obey the LORD or carry out his fierce wrath against the Amalekites, the LORD has done this to you today. [19]The LORD will deliver both Israel and you into the hands of the Philistines, and tomorrow you and your sons will be with me.

Eternal life in the Old Testament

The idea of an eternal life is also present within the old testament in such passages as Daniel 12:2, Psalm 16: 9-11, 49:15, 73:24 Isaiah 26:10 Dan12: 1-2. These ideas developed over time, leading in the end to a clear belief in the resurrection of the dead and the afterlife. These beliefs continued to develop within the intertestamental period. (see references below)

Daniel 12:2

Multitudes who sleep in the dust of the earth will awake: some to everlasting life, others to shame and everlasting contempt.

Psalm 16:9-11

[9]Therefore my heart is glad and my tongue rejoices; my body also will rest secure, [10] because you will not abandon me to the realm of the dead, nor will you let your faithful [h] one see decay. [11]You make known to me the path of life; you will fill me with joy in your presence, with eternal pleasures at your right hand.

Psalm 49:15

But God will redeem me from the realm of the dead; he will surely take me to himself.

Psalm 73:24

You guide me with your counsel, and afterward you will take me into glory.

The concept of a Resurrection Body and life in the age to come:

Isaiah 26:19

But your dead will live, Lord; their bodies will rise— let those who dwell in the dust wake up and shout for joy— your dew is like the dew of the morning; the earth will give birth to her dead.

Daniel 12:1-2

The Dead Will Rise to Life

"At that time Michael, the great prince who protects your people, will arise. There will be a time of distress such as has not happened from the beginning of nations until then. But at that time your people—everyone whose name is found written in the book—will be delivered. [2]Multitudes who sleep in the dust of the earth will awake: some to everlasting life, others to shame and everlasting contempt.

These images of a resurrection after death led in Jewish thought to the whole idea of Sheol, a waiting 'state' which would exist after physical death. Sheol is seen as either, a place of suffering for those who are the wicked or alternatively as a place of resurrection for the righteous to an eternal life with God.

Eternal Life within the Gospels.

When we come to the idea of eternal life within the Gospels it is important to note straight away that whilst all 4 Gospels clearly show Jesus talking about eternal life, Johns Gospel has a somewhat different emphasis.

John stresses the presence of this eternal life NOW, that is, in this life. For John this gift of eternal life is 'realised' in eschatological terms, that is, it is present and active within the lives of Christians as soon as they discover faith in Jesus. Eternal life then is a present, active and living reality which continues within the experience of believers after the die.

In the synoptic gospels the focus of Jesus teaching on eternal life is almost entirely on the eschatological (end time) nature of eternal life.

These differences however, far from being contradictory, complement each other creating an extremely exciting picture of the eternal life which Faith in Jesus creates.

John's emphasis on the 'realisation' of this eternal spiritual life within the present experience of Christians is, in my view, fundamentally important in our quest to discover some sort of assurance of salvation. I will return to it in a moment.

Eternal life in the Synoptic Gospels

In the synoptic gospels then, we find Jesus teaching and talking about eternal life on numerous occasions. (See examples below)

Mark Chapter 10 vs 17-29

A Rich Man

17As Jesus started on his way, a man ran up to him and fell on his knees before him. "Good teacher," he asked, "what must I do to inherit eternal life?"

18 "Why do you call me good?" Jesus answered. "No one is good—except God alone. 19You know the commandments: 'You shall not murder, you shall not commit adultery, you shall not steal, you shall not give false testimony, you shall not defraud, honor your father and mother.'[d]"

20 "Teacher," he declared, "all these I have kept since I was a boy."

21 Jesus looked at him and loved him. "One thing you lack," he said. "Go, sell everything you have and give to the poor, and you will have treasure in heaven. Then come, follow me."

22At this the man's face fell. He went away sad, because he had great wealth.

23Jesus looked around and said to his disciples, "How hard it is for the rich to enter the kingdom of God!"

24 The disciples were amazed at his words. But Jesus said again, "Children, how hard it is [e] to enter the kingdom of God! 25It is easier for a camel to go through the eye of a needle than for someone who is rich to enter the kingdom of God."

26The disciples were even more amazed, and said to each other, "Who then can be saved?"

27Jesus looked at them and said, "With man this is impossible, but not with God; all things are possible with God."

²⁸ Then Peter spoke up, "We have left everything to follow you!"

²⁹ "Truly I tell you," Jesus replied, "no one who has left home or brothers or sisters or mother or father or children or fields for me and the gospel ³⁰will fail to receive a hundred times as much in this present age: homes, brothers, sisters, mothers, children and fields—along with persecutions—and in the age to come eternal life. ³¹But many who are first will be last, and the last first."

Matthew 25:46

"Then they will go away to eternal punishment, but the righteous to eternal life."

Matthew 7:13,14

¹³"Enter through the narrow gate. For wide is the gate and broad is the road that leads to destruction, and many enter through it. ¹⁴But small is the gate and narrow the road that leads to life, and only a few find it.

Mark 9:43-47

⁴³If your hand causes you to stumble, cut it off. It is better for you to enter life maimed than with two hands to go into hell, where the fire never goes out.[44] ⁴⁵And if your foot causes you to stumble, cut it off. It is better for you to enter life crippled than to have two feet and be thrown into hell. [46] ⁴⁷And if your eye causes you to stumble, pluck it out. It is better for you to enter the kingdom of God with one eye than to have two eyes and be thrown into hell,

The Good Samaritan – Luke chapter 10 vs 25-28

²⁵On one occasion an expert in the law stood up to test Jesus. "Teacher," he asked, "what must I do to inherit eternal life?"²⁶"What is written in the Law?" he replied. "How do you read it?"²⁷He answered, "'Love the Lord your God with all your heart and with all your soul and with all your strength and with all your mind'[c]; and, 'Love your neighbour as yourself.'²⁸"You have answered correctly," Jesus replied. "Do this and you will live."

Eternal life then within the synoptics is a future event, which will occur at the end of time, in the world that is yet to come. This fits well with the picture of such things as a last Judgment, the dead rising and 'all that jazz' as we say.

Johns Gospel

In John's gospel, as already explained, we find a different emphasis. The idea of the end time resurrection to eternal life is not missing. Some of the passages in John clearly express both the present and the future aspects of eternal life however, as we have said, the emphasis on its presence now is clearly foremost in Johns mind.

Passages in John's Gospel which express both the present and future aspects of eternal life.

John Chapter 5 vs 19 – 39.

19 Jesus gave them this answer: "Very truly I tell you, the Son can do nothing by himself; he can do only what he sees his Father doing, because whatever the Father does the Son also does. 20 For the Father loves the Son and shows him all he does. Yes, and he will show him even greater works than these, so that you will be amazed. 21For just as the Father raises the dead and gives them life, even so the Son gives life to whom he is pleased to give it. 22Moreover, the Father judges no one, but has entrusted all judgment to the Son, 23that all may honor the Son just as they honor the Father. Whoever does not honor the Son does not honor the Father, who sent him.

24 "Very truly I tell you, whoever hears my word and believes him who sent me has eternal life and will not be judged but has crossed over from death to life. 25Very truly I tell you, a time is coming and has now come when the dead will hear the voice of the Son of God and those who hear will live. 26For as the Father has life in himself, so he has granted the Son also to have life in himself. 27And he has given him authority to judge because he is the Son of Man.

28 "Do not be amazed at this, for a time is coming when all who are in their graves will hear his voice 29and come out—those who have done what is good will rise to live, and those who have done what is evil will rise to be condemned. 30By myself I can do nothing; I judge only as I hear, and my judgment is just, for I seek not to please myself but him who sent me.

Testimonies About Jesus

31 "If I testify about myself, my testimony is not true. 32 There is another who testifies in my favor, and I know that his testimony about me is true.

33 "You have sent to John and he has testified to the truth. 34Not that I accept human testimony; but I mention it that you may be saved. 35John was a lamp that burned and gave light, and you chose for a time to enjoy his light.

36"I have testimony weightier than that of John. For the works that the Father has given me to finish—the very works that I am doing—testify that the Father has sent me. 37And the Father who sent me has himself testified concerning me. You have never heard his voice nor seen his form, 38nor does his word dwell in you, for you do not believe the one he sent. 39You study [c] the Scriptures diligently because you think that in them you have eternal life. These are the very Scriptures that testify about me, 40yet you refuse to come to me to have life.

John Chapter 3 vs 31- 36.

The One Who Comes from Heaven.

31 The one who comes from above is above all; the one who is from the earth belongs to the earth, and speaks as one from the earth. The one who comes from heaven is above all. 32 He testifies to what he has seen and heard, but no one accepts his testimony. 33 Whoever has accepted it has certified that God is truthful. 34 For the one whom God has sent speaks the words of God, for God[i] gives the Spirit without limit. 35 The Father loves the Son and has placed everything in his hands. 36 Whoever believes in the Son has eternal life, but whoever rejects the Son will not see life, for God's wrath remains on them.

Passages which stress the Present experience of eternal life:

John 10 vs 10

10 The thief comes only to steal and kill and destroy; I have come that they may have life and have it to the full.

John 6:33

33 For the bread of God is the bread that comes down from heaven and gives life to the world."

John 6:35

then Jesus declared, "I am the bread of life. Whoever comes to me will never go hungry, and whoever believes in me will never be thirsty.

John 6:63

The Spirit gives life; the flesh counts for nothing. The words I have spoken to you—they are full of the Spirit[e] and life.

John 5:21 and 26

21 For just as the Father raises the dead and gives them life, even so the Son gives life to whom he is pleased to give it.

26 For as the Father has life in himself, so he has granted the Son also to have life in himself.

John 4:10

10 Jesus answered her, "If you knew the gift of God and who it is that asks you for a drink, you would have asked him and he would have given you living water."

John 4:14

14 but whoever drinks the water I give them will never thirst. Indeed, the water I give them will become in them a spring of water welling up to eternal life."

John 10:28

28 I give them eternal life, and they shall never perish; no one will snatch them out of my hand.

John 11:25-26

25 Jesus said to her, "I am the resurrection and the life. The one who believes in me will live, even though they die; 26and whoever lives by believing in me will never die. Do you believe this?"

Understanding this dualism

Earlier on in this book you will remember that we thought a little about the idea of the Kingdom of God and its 'realised' presence. The idea that through the life, ministry, death and resurrection of Jesus certain aspects of the 'coming end time Kingdom of God' had thrust their way into history, impacting on our lives. You will remember the debate between the two theologians Wiess and Switzer; one who argued that everything that belonged to the Kingdom of God would come into being at the end of time, while the other, that everything that belonged to the end time Kingdom of God had already arrived in Jesus' ministry and could now be accessed by people through faith.

We concluded that what the Gospels actually reflect is a compromise between these two views. That whilst some of the blessings of the kingdom were clearly taught by Jesus to have arrived now, like forgiveness for example, others would only become accessible once Christ returned and the New Age was consummated in its fullness. Our complete healing, the end of all evil, sin, pain, and suffering being some examples of these end of time blessings.

It seems that here, in this contrast between the Synoptics and John's gospel the same tension is apparent. In the 3 Synoptic Gospels we find Jesus pointing us towards the consummation of the Kingdom of God and eternal life at the end of time. Whereas, in John, we discover that Jesus taught that even though there would be a day when the dead will rise to eternal life within the new kingdom, the experience of this same eschatological (end time) eternal life has also arrived now. In essence we already live within and experience the presence of this promised eternal life now. We find the source of this experience is found within Jesus himself; that his mission was to bring this experience into the world now and this experience is the guarantee that we will rise at the end of the age.

This is incredibly exciting because it means that in my present experience of Jesus; in my present experience of the indwelling of the Holy Spirit; in the present experience of that new birth 40 years ago, which made me spiritually alive and aware of God, an experience that despite my fears of death I find impossible to deny, I am experiencing already a foretaste of my future eternal life.

Anecdotally, I can remember vividly, whilst at the London Bible College I was struck down one day with one of the panic attacks I mentioned at the beginning of this chapter. Still reeling from this attack I attended a lecture on the Old Testament and as I sat in my seat still rather shaken, the lecturer opened with these words "Physical death can in no way interrupt our spiritual life in Jesus" I was stunned at this coincidence and instantly comforted by the words. I felt that God had kicked me up the behind and was telling me to frankly just get a grip.

The lesson we must learn from John's emphasis is simply that we do not live as Christians in an empty waiting place, longing to receive what Jesus promised. The blessings of the Kingdom have become a reality within our lives already through the giving of the Spirit at Pentecost. We have been re-born; we are already Spiritual beings in Christ; we have received those elements of the future coming kingdom that we need in order to be saved. We have been given the Spirit as the seal and promise of our future in Christ. We have already experienced and are experiencing eternal life and in this experience, we can find hope that in the end, when we die, we will rise again with Jesus into the end- time eternal life of the kingdom of God when it is finally consummated.

This theology is reflected within other New Testament passages:

Galatians 6:8

8 Whoever sows to please their flesh, from the flesh will reap destruction; whoever sows to please the Spirit, from the Spirit will reap eternal life.

Romans 6:23

23 For the wages of sin is death, but the gift of God is eternal life in Christ Jesus our Lord.

1 Timothy 1:16

16 But for that very reason I was shown mercy so that in me, the worst of sinners, Christ Jesus might display his immense patience as an example for those who would believe in him and receive eternal life.

1 Timothy 6:12

12 Fight the good fight of the faith. Take hold of the eternal life to which you were called when you made your good confession in the presence of many witnesses.

1 John 1 vs1-4

The Incarnation of the Word of Life

1 That which was from the beginning, which we have heard, which we have seen with our eyes, which we have looked at and our hands have touched—this we proclaim concerning the Word of life. ² The life appeared; we have seen it and testify to it, and we proclaim to you the eternal life, which was with the Father and has appeared to us. ³ We proclaim to you what we have seen and heard, so that you also may have fellowship with us. And our fellowship is with the Father and with his Son, Jesus Christ. ⁴ We write this to make our[a] joy complete.

Resurrection within the New Testament.

Finally, we cannot leave this section without reference to the idea of resurrection and in particular to the resurrection of Jesus himself. In these events we see the historical and physical witness to our own eternal hope.

While he was alive Jesus claimed to have the power to defeat death, biblically speaking, the ultimate victory that evil has over God's creation.

Years ago, when I was the Vicar of my first Parish Church in north west London, I had two rather extraordinary ladies from Eastern Europe who started to attend our Sunday morning worship services. Both of these dear ladies were pretty elderly. The younger one looked to be around 75 at least and the older probably well into her 80's or even 90's. They always arrived together having walked for about one and a half miles from their home on the 15th floor of one of the local tower blocks. I assumed at first they were sisters.

Whilst attending worship, I noticed that each Sunday the younger one would whisper to the older constantly throughout our services. I discovered that the older lady spoke no English at all, the younger was translating every word of the service for her.

As time passed, I discovered that the older lady was in fact her mother and was well into her 90's and it became very obvious that the daughter's whole life had, for a number of years, become completely centred around her care.

A couple of years went by and as sadly happens the mother got quite poorly and was taken into hospital. Her daughter became obsessed with her care and on one occasion tried to smuggle her mother out of the hospital in the dead of night. In what could only be described as a sort of midnight Ninja raid, wheelchair in hand, she broke into the ward and was caught trying to wheel her Mother out. The police were called, the daughter taken home, and Mum was returned back to the ward.

A few weeks after that I received a phone call from the daughter.

'Father', she said to me, 'you must come, mother has died' I naturally expressed my condolences and asked when she had died. 'Two weeks ago,' came the reply 'She still in bed you come!' Having been a police officer for 25 years by then, I was well aware of what was likely to face me. I went to the flat and sure enough there was Mother dead and lying-in state. 'Now' said the daughter 'You pray, you raise her from the dead like Lazarus'. Well, I thought, that's a first. Give it a go! Nothing ventured and all that! After all this could be a career changer for me!

I, of course instead, explained to the daughter that I didn't really feel that this was a likely outcome of any such prayers. I talked to her rather about that fact that her Mum was now at peace with Jesus and alive with him in her Spirit in a far better place.

There were, of course, a number of difficult emotions going on within that situation. Emotions of loss, of emptiness and of grief, but one of them also revolved, for the bereaved daughter, around the question of trust. Trust that is in the very meaning and efficacy of the promises of our Christian Faith. A faith that as we have already shown above, promises us a security of eternal life within the grace and love of God in Jesus when we die.

John 11 vs 38 – 44 The raising of Lazarus from the dead.

Now we know from the Gospels that Lazarus wasn't the first Person that Jesus had raised from the dead. He had also raised Jairus's daughter, recorded in Marks Gospel chapter 5 and the widow's son at Nain, recorded in Luke chapter 7. But it is clear that the raising of Lazarus is significantly different because, according to the accounts that we have Lazarus had been dead for 4 days. To suggest then that Lazarus had been unconscious or simply sick fails to accord with the evidence which likewise, clearly suggests (due to the presence of the bad smell) that he had already started to decompose! This was then according to all the evidence a supernatural event. In this Jesus demonstrated his power to accomplish that which he claimed he had come to do, that is, to bring new life, to defeat the power of death over humanity and raise men and women to new spiritual and physical, eternal life. Jesus had, in fact, waited for two extra days after hearing of his friend's death just so he could demonstrate these truths. He wanted his followers to know that faith in him was and is essentially faith in the one who comes as the vanquisher of death. This death that came into the world and stalks us all because of the corruption of sin. It was, and is, the proof that all he had said about his mission to save mankind was true. The emotion which Jesus is recorded as experiencing can be understood in the original text in terms of anger, of him being, if you like 'enraged'. As indignation in the face of Lazarus's death. Here, then, we see Jesus face to face with his greatest enemy, the final enemy that as the Apostle Paul puts it, he has come to destroy (1 Corinthians 15).

B.B. Warfield comments on this – "It is death itself that is the object of Christ's wrath here, tears of sympathy may fill his eyes, but this is incidental as his Soul is held by rage and he advances to the Tomb, as Calvin says – 'As a Champion who prepares for conflict".

The raising of Lazarus then becomes a definitive act, a decisive moment, a moment of victory and of hope for us all.

So, for those of us who find such things difficult to believe 2000 years later, we should take great comfort, solace and hope from the fact that those who were there were in absolutely no doubt about what had happened. They were so convinced by what they witnessed first-hand that many of them, including the disciples themselves, were prepared to go to the most horrible of deaths without recanting the faith that came into being, in a great part, because of their witness of this event.

I simply ask would they, if they knew it was untrue, have submitted themselves to crucifixion and martyrdom in such places as the Colosseum at Rome? Would you? Would I? I doubt it. They knew, they had seen, and they believed without any doubt that Jesus had accomplished this incredible miracle.

The Resurrection of Jesus:

The importance of Christ's own Resurrection for the Christian faith cannot really be overstated as the Apostle Paul himself tells us in

1 Corinthians chapter 15 vs 12-32

[12] But if it is preached that Christ has been raised from the dead, how can some of you say that there is no resurrection of the dead? [13] If there is no resurrection of the dead, then not even Christ has been raised. [14] And if Christ has not been raised, our preaching is useless and so is your faith. [15] More than that, we are then found to be false witnesses about God, for we have testified about God that he raised Christ from the dead. But he did not raise him if in fact the dead are

not raised. [16]For if the dead are not raised, then Christ has not been raised either. [17]And if Christ has not been raised, your faith is futile; you are still in your sins. [18]Then those also who have fallen asleep in Christ are lost. [19]If only for this life we have hope in Christ, we are of all people most to be pitied.

[20]But Christ has indeed been raised from the dead, the firstfruits of those who have fallen asleep. [21]For since death came through a man, the resurrection of the dead comes also through a man. [22]For as in Adam all die, so in Christ all will be made alive. [23]But each in turn: Christ, the firstfruits; then, when he comes, those who belong to him. [24]Then the end will come, when he hands over the kingdom to God the Father after he has destroyed all dominion, authority and power. [25]For he must reign until he has put all his enemies under his feet. [26]The last enemy to be destroyed is death. [27]For he "has put everything under his feet."[c] Now when it says that "everything" has been put under him, it is clear that this does not include God himself, who put everything under Christ. [28]When he has done this, then the Son himself will be made subject to him who put everything under him, so that God may be all in all.

[29]Now if there is no resurrection, what will those do who are baptized for the dead? If the dead are not raised at all, why are people baptized for them? [30]And as for us, why do we endanger ourselves every hour? [31]I face death every day— yes, just as surely as I boast about you in Christ Jesus our Lord. [32]If I fought wild beasts in Ephesus with no more than human hopes, what have I gained? If the dead are not raised,

The resurrection of Jesus Christ is the one fact on which the Christian hope stands or falls. In this victory over death Christ undid the consequences of Adam's sin, the first rebellion which, as we discussed earlier in our chapter on the problem of evil, brought the malignant power of sin and death into God's creation "For as in Adam all die, so also in Christ all will be made alive".

In **1 Corinthians chapter 15 vs 3-8** The Apostle Paul writes:

[3]For what I received I passed on to you as of first importance[a]: that Christ died for our sins according to the Scriptures, [4]that he was buried, that he was raised on the third day according to the Scriptures, [5]and that he appeared to Cephas,[b] and then to the Twelve. [6]After that, he appeared to more than five hundred of the brothers and sisters at the same time, most of whom are still

living, though some have fallen asleep. ⁷Then he appeared to James, then to all the apostles, ⁸and last of all he appeared to me also, as to one abnormally born.

We also have numerous other eyewitness accounts of Christ's Resurrection appearances within the Gospel accounts. For example, in Mark's Gospel after Mary discovers the empty tomb and is instructed by the Angels to tell the disciples Jesus has risen from the dead, Jesus appears to her. Then later to the disciples, where he proclaims their great commission.

Mark 16:10-16

⁹When Jesus rose early on the first day of the week, he appeared first to Mary Magdalene, out of whom he had driven seven demons. ¹⁰She went and told those who had been with him and who were mourning and weeping. ¹¹When they heard that Jesus was alive and that she had seen him, they did not believe it.

¹²Afterward Jesus appeared in a different form to two of them while they were walking in the country. ¹³These returned and reported it to the rest; but they did not believe them either.

¹⁴Later Jesus appeared to the Eleven as they were eating; he rebuked them for their lack of faith and their stubborn refusal to believe those who had seen him after he had risen.

¹⁵He said to them, "Go into all the world and preach the gospel to all creation. ¹⁶Whoever believes and is baptized will be saved, but whoever does not believe will be condemned.

In Matthew, Luke and John's Gospels Jesus appears to Mary, then to the disciples. There are also appearances in Galilee and Jerusalem. In Luke Jesus appears and ascends to heaven near Bethany.

Luke 24 vs 24 – 53.

²⁴Then some of our companions went to the tomb and found it just as the women had said, but they did not see Jesus."

²⁵He said to them, "How foolish you are, and how slow to believe all that the prophets have spoken! ²⁶Did not the Messiah have to suffer these things and then enter his glory?" *27* And beginning with Moses and all the Prophets, he explained to them what was said in all the Scriptures concerning himself.

28 As they approached the village to which they were going, Jesus continued on as if he were going farther. *29* But they urged him strongly, "Stay with us, for it is nearly evening; the day is almost over." So he went in to stay with them.

30 When he was at the table with them, he took bread, gave thanks, broke it and began to give it to them. *31* Then their eyes were opened and they recognized him, and he disappeared from their sight. *32* They asked each other, "Were not our hearts burning within us while he talked with us on the road and opened the Scriptures to us?"

33 They got up and returned at once to Jerusalem. There they found the Eleven and those with them, assembled together *34* and saying, "It is true! The Lord has risen and has appeared to Simon." *35* Then the two told what had happened on the way, and how Jesus was recognized by them when he broke the bread.

Jesus Appears to the Disciples

36 While they were still talking about this, Jesus himself stood among them and said to them, "Peace be with you."

37 They were startled and frightened, thinking they saw a ghost. *38* He said to them, "Why are you troubled, and why do doubts rise in your minds? *39* Look at my hands and my feet. It is I myself! Touch me and see; a ghost does not have flesh and bones, as you see I have."

40 When he had said this, he showed them his hands and feet. *41* And while they still did not believe it because of joy and amazement, he asked them, "Do you have anything here to eat?" *42* They gave him a piece of broiled fish, *43* and he took it and ate it in their presence.

44 He said to them, "This is what I told you while I was still with you: Everything must be fulfilled that is written about me in the Law of Moses, the Prophets and the Psalms."

45 Then he opened their minds so they could understand the Scriptures. *46* He told them, "This is what is written: The Messiah will suffer and rise from the *dead on the third day, [47] and repentance for the forgiveness of sins will be preached in his name to all nations, beginning at Jerusalem. [48] You are witnesses of these things. [49] I am going to send you what my Father has promised; but stay in the city until you have been clothed with power from on high."*

The Ascension of Jesus

[50] When he had led them out to the vicinity of Bethany, he lifted up his hands and blessed them. [51] While he was blessing them, he left them and was taken up into heaven. [52] Then they worshiped him and returned to Jerusalem with great joy. [53] And they stayed continually at the temple, praising God.

The book of Acts states, that Jesus continued to appear to his followers for 40 days until the Ascension.

In Johns gospel Mary finds the empty tomb and tells Peter. After this Jesus appears to her and then to Peter, Thomas and the other disciples while they are fishing.

John 21:1-19

Jesus and the Miraculous Catch of Fish

21 Afterward Jesus appeared again to his disciples, by the Sea of Galilee.[a] It happened this way: [2] Simon Peter, Thomas (also known as Didymus[b]), Nathanael from Cana in Galilee, the sons of Zebedee, and two other disciples were together. [3] "I'm going out to fish," Simon Peter told them, and they said, "We'll go with you." So they went out and got into the boat, but that night they caught nothing.

[4] Early in the morning, Jesus stood on the shore, but the disciples did not realize that it was Jesus.

[5] He called out to them, "Friends, haven't you any fish?"

"No," they answered.

[6] He said, "Throw your net on the right side of the boat and you will find some." When they did, they were unable to haul the net in because of the large number of fish.

[7] Then the disciple whom Jesus loved said to Peter, "It is the Lord!" As soon as Simon Peter heard him say, "It is the Lord," he wrapped his outer garment

around him (for he had taken it off) and jumped into the water. [8] The other disciples followed in the boat, towing the net full of fish, for they were not far from shore, about a hundred yards.[c] [9] When they landed, they saw a fire of burning coals there with fish on it, and some bread.

[10] Jesus said to them, "Bring some of the fish you have just caught." [11] So Simon Peter climbed back into the boat and dragged the net ashore. It was full of large fish, 153, but even with so many the net was not torn. [12] Jesus said to them, "Come and have breakfast." None of the disciples dared ask him, "Who are you?" They knew it was the Lord. [13] Jesus came, took the bread and gave it to them, and did the same with the fish. [14] This was now the third time Jesus appeared to his disciples after he was raised from the dead.

Jesus Reinstates Peter

[15] When they had finished eating, Jesus said to Simon Peter, "Simon son of John, do you love me more than these?"

"Yes, Lord," he said, "you know that I love you."

Jesus said, "Feed my lambs."

[16] Again Jesus said, "Simon son of John, do you love me?"

He answered, "Yes, Lord, you know that I love you."

Jesus said, "Take care of my sheep."

[17] The third time he said to him, "Simon son of John, do you love me?"

Peter was hurt because Jesus asked him the third time, "Do you love me?" He said, "Lord, you know all things; you know that I love you."

Jesus said, "Feed my sheep. [18] Very truly I tell you, when you were younger you dressed yourself and went where you wanted; but when you are old you will stretch out your hands, and someone else will dress you and lead you where you do not want to go." [19] Jesus said this to indicate the kind of death by which Peter would glorify God. Then he said to him, "Follow me!"

Again, for those who might doubt the validity or honesty of these accounts, we must, as above remember, that those who claim to have seen these things were so convinced that even the most severe torture and martyrdom failed to convince any of them to recant their stories. Regardless of how we view these claims those who made them were clearly willing to literally put their lives on the line, rather than recant. This certainly seems somewhat convincing to me.

The Conversion of the Apostle Paul.

Whilst I was studying theology at the London Bible College, I found myself going through something of a crisis of faith. This crisis revolved around my own belief in the resurrection. As I pondered these stories and considered their validity, I was struck most of all by the witness of Saint Paul. Here was a man originally set absolutely against the early Church's claims about Jesus. He was a highly educated Pharisee and a zealot for the cause of Israel. He persecuted the early Church with the one aim of destroying the Christian faith. He was responsible for terrible persecutions. He in no way could have ever been described as someone who had any reason, sympathy or motivation to promote the idea that Jesus had risen from the dead. Paul's conversion is as convincing a story as one could ever wish to read.

The Conversion of Saul Acts Chapter 9

Saul's Conversion

9 Meanwhile, Saul was still breathing out murderous threats against the Lord's disciples. He went to the high priest [2] and asked him for letters to the synagogues in Damascus, so that if he found any there who belonged to the Way, whether men or women, he might take them as prisoners to Jerusalem. [3] As he neared Damascus on his journey, suddenly a light from heaven flashed around him. [4] He fell to the ground and heard a voice say to him, "Saul, Saul, why do you persecute me?"

[5] "Who are you, Lord?" Saul asked.

"I am Jesus, whom you are persecuting," he replied. [6] "Now get up and go into the city, and you will be told what you must do."

[7] The men traveling with Saul stood there speechless; they heard the sound but did not see anyone. [8] Saul got up from the ground, but when he opened his eyes he could see nothing. So they led him by the hand into Damascus. [9] For three days he was blind, and did not eat or drink anything.

¹⁰ In Damascus there was a disciple named Ananias. The Lord called to him in a vision, "Ananias!"

"Yes, Lord," he answered.

¹¹ The Lord told him, "Go to the house of Judas on Straight Street and ask for a man from Tarsus named Saul, for he is praying. ¹² In a vision he has seen a man named Ananias come and place his hands on him to restore his sight."

¹³ "Lord," Ananias answered, "I have heard many reports about this man and all the harm he has done to your holy people in Jerusalem. ¹⁴ And he has come here with authority from the chief priests to arrest all who call on your name."

¹⁵ But the Lord said to Ananias, "Go! This man is my chosen instrument to proclaim my name to the Gentiles and their kings and to the people of Israel. ¹⁶ I will show him how much he must suffer for my name."

¹⁷ Then Ananias went to the house and entered it. Placing his hands on Saul, he said, "Brother Saul, the Lord—Jesus, who appeared to you on the road as you were coming here—has sent me so that you may see again and be filled with the Holy Spirit." ¹⁸ Immediately, something like scales fell from Saul's eyes, and he could see again. He got up and was baptized, ¹⁹ and after taking some food, he regained his strength.

Saul in Damascus and Jerusalem

Saul spent several days with the disciples in Damascus. ²⁰ At once he began to preach in the synagogues that Jesus is the Son of God. ²¹ All those who heard him were astonished and asked, "Isn't he the man who raised havoc in Jerusalem among those who call on this name? And hasn't he come here to take them as prisoners to the chief priests?" ²² Yet Saul grew more and more powerful and baffled the Jews living in Damascus by proving that Jesus is the Messiah.

²³ After many days had gone by, there was a conspiracy among the Jews to kill him, ²⁴ but Saul learned of their plan. Day and night they kept close watch on the city gates in order to kill him. ²⁵ But his followers took him by night and lowered him in a basket through an opening in the wall.

26 When he came to Jerusalem, he tried to join the disciples, but they were all afraid of him, not believing that he really was a disciple. 27 But Barnabas took him and brought him to the apostles. He told them how Saul on his journey had seen the Lord and that the Lord had spoken to him, and how in Damascus he had preached fearlessly in the name of Jesus. 28 So Saul stayed with them and moved about freely in Jerusalem, speaking boldly in the name of the Lord. 29 He talked and debated with the Hellenistic Jews,[a] but they tried to kill him. 30 When the believers learned of this, they took him down to Caesarea and sent him off to Tarsus.

31 Then the church throughout Judea, Galilee and Samaria enjoyed a time of peace and was strengthened. Living in the fear of the Lord and encouraged by the Holy Spirit, it increased in numbers.

I find this story and the subsequent change in Paul's life from persecutor to the early Church's greatest Apostle; his willingness to die for his faith in the Colosseum at Rome, to be utterly convincing. The important point to note here for the purpose of this chapter is that Paul does not say in his story that he received a vision of Jesus. He states that he met the risen Christ in person. He became an Apostle, the 'least of the Apostles', in his own words because the risen Christ appeared to him last, 'as one abnormally born'. A vision may not have been as convincing but meeting Jesus in person clearly was.

Saul had no predetermined Christian agenda; no reason to change his views; no belief whatsoever in the stories of the first disciples. His one purpose at the point of his conversion was to get rid of them, to destroy the Christian witness and rid Judaism of this heretical sect.

It seems to be utterly reasonable to say from this evidence that those who testify to the resurrection were utterly convinced of the truthfulness of their experience. This was no plot to 'resurrect' a dying faith; no attempt at subterfuge; no dishonesty can be applied. This should give us a sincere assurance that Jesus indeed rose from the dead and appeared to these witnesses and that they were utterly convinced that this same Jesus was the Resurrected, Divine Son of God.

In summary, then, the gift of eternal life is the ultimate promise of our faith. It is a gift that can be demonstrated through our experience of spiritual life now; through the witness of the Gospel stories, through the testimonies of the original disciples and through the utterly convincing testimony and life of the Apostle Paul, all of whom were willing to die rather than to recant their claims.

This must surely give us a firm ground for hope in the truth of our faith and the promise that our own 'resurrection life' will continue beyond our physical death.

Chapter 9

The Holy Spirit and His role

In my own experience over the past 30 years the subject of the Holy Spirit and his role within the Church has been by far the most controversial and divisive subject amongst both individual Christians and within Church communities. This has been the case for me perhaps, because for most of my Christian life up until I began my training for the Anglican Priesthood, I had always been involved in what Christians call the Charismatic Church. (The 'happy, clappy' type, as many non-Charismatics call them.)

Charismatics are, in general terms, Christians who believe the following about the role of the Holy Spirit within the life of the Church.

(1) The Holy Spirit brings into people's lives the 'new spiritual birth' which Jesus talks about to Nicodemus in John's Gospel Chapter 3.

(2) That it is the role of the Spirit to then 'FILL' Christians / the Church with his presence. This in turn brings into Christians lives and therefore the Church the gifts and ministries of God's kingdom. These include, the miraculous, signs and wonders along with all the other more generally recognised ministries such as preaching, teaching etc.

In basic terms Charismatics see the Holy Spirit as the author of the 'new kingdom spiritual life' of the Church on earth and the communicator of God the Father's presence and power.

The Holy Spirit is the third person of the Trinity (the three persons of God) and it is he who has come to the Church since Pentecost to continue, through the Church, the ministry of the Kingdom. He replaces Jesus as the Presence of the almighty God on earth in and through his Church, which becomes, because of his presence, the place where God now lives, breathes and has his being.

The Holy Spirit is the one who initiates, sustains and empowers Christians' individual and corporate life within their relationship to God. I completely agree with all these statements. This is what I believe the N/T teaches and this has also been and still is consistent with my own personal experience.

In the Gospel of John Jesus is recorded as formulating what we should rightly call the first New Testament theology of the Holy Spirit. In John 14 Jesus, when talking about his coming death comforts his disciples by saying "If you love me, you will obey my commands and I will ask the Father and he will give you another counsellor, to be with you, the Spirit of truth". Later Jesus also says "I will not leave you as orphans, I will come back to you".

Jesus Promises the Holy Spirit

John chapter 14 vs 15-21

Jesus Promises the Holy Spirit

[15] *"If you love me, keep my commands. [16] And I will ask the Father, and he will give you another advocate to help you and be with you forever— [17] the Spirit of truth. The world cannot accept him, because it neither sees him nor knows him. But you know him, for he lives with you and will be[c] in you. [18] I will not leave you as orphans; I will come to you. [19] Before long, the world will not see me anymore, but you will see me. Because I live, you also will live. [20] On that day you will realize that I am in my Father, and you are in me, and I am in you. [21] Whoever has my commands and keeps them is the one who loves me. The one who loves me will be loved by my Father, and I too will love them and show myself to them."*

[25] *"All this I have spoken while still with you. 26 But the Advocate, the Holy Spirit, whom the Father will send in my name, will teach you all things and will remind you of everything I have said to you.*

Jesus clearly appears to be suggesting that, essentially, the role of the Spirit in the lives of believers will be (as suggested above) to replace Jesus within his disciple's lives and continue the kingdom ministry he started, through them on earth. It seems perfectly fair to me, to suggest in light of this, that the continuing ministry of the Church should potentially contain ALL the aspects of the ministry of Christ, whether that is the preaching of the Gospel, the communication of God's love and forgiveness, the ministry of the sacraments or indeed, the miracles, signs and wonders! Personally, I haven't ever come across any reasonable argument for saying anything else. This was also clearly the experience of the early Church as recorded in Luke's 'Acts of the

Apostles' post Pentecost and has remained so in the experience of many Christian Churches up until the present day.

Paul's writings:

In the writings of the Apostle Paul the role of the Spirit within the lives of believers is expanded to explain how the presence of the Spirit affects believer's lives.

For example;

- The Spirit's presence within our lives makes us God's children, i.e. initiates our adoption.

- He transforms us, that is, by his influence we grow to become more like God.

- We become 'New creations', that is, spiritual beings through the presence of the Spirit.

- He communicates the presence and grace of God the Father into our lives.

The Apostle expresses these beliefs in a variety of passages some of which I have evidenced below.

1 Corinthians 3:16

Don't you know that you yourselves are God's temple and that God's Spirit dwells in your midst?

1 Corinthians 2:10-11

[10] these are the things God has revealed to us by his Spirit. The Spirit searches all things, even the deep things of God. [11] For who knows a person's thoughts except their own spirit within them? In the same way no one knows the thoughts of God except the Spirit of God.

Ephesians 1:17-20

[17] I keep asking that the God of our Lord Jesus Christ, the glorious Father, may give you the Spirit of wisdom and revelation, so that you may know him better. [18] I pray that the eyes of your heart may be enlightened in order that you may know the hope to which he has called you, the riches of his glorious inheritance in his holy people, [19] and his incomparably great power for us who believe. That power is the same as the mighty strength [20] he exerted when he

raised Christ from the dead and seated him at his right hand in the heavenly realms.

1 Corinthians 12:7-11

7Now to each one the manifestation of the Spirit is given for the common good. 8To one there is given through the Spirit a message of wisdom, to another a message of knowledge by means of the same Spirit, 9to another faith by the same Spirit, to another gifts of healing by that one Spirit, 10to another miraculous powers, to another prophecy, to another distinguishing between spirits, to another speaking in different kinds of tongues, and to still another the interpretation of tongues. 11All these are the work of one and the same Spirit, and he distributes them to each one, just as he determines.

Ephesians 1:13 -14

13And you also were included in Christ when you heard the message of truth, the gospel of your salvation. When you believed, you were marked in him with a seal, the promised Holy Spirit, 14who is a deposit guaranteeing our inheritance until the redemption of those who are God's possession—to the praise of his glory.

Romans 8 vs 1 – 17

Life Through the Spirit

8 Therefore, there is now no condemnation for those who are in Christ Jesus, 2 because through Christ Jesus the law of the Spirit who gives life has set you[a] free from the law of sin and death. 3 For what the law was powerless to do because it was weakened by the flesh,[b] God did by sending his own Son in the likeness of sinful flesh to be a sin offering.[c] And so he condemned sin in the flesh, 4 in order that the righteous requirement of the law might be fully met in us, who do not live according to the flesh but according to the Spirit.

5 Those who live according to the flesh have their minds set on what the flesh desires; but those who live in accordance with the Spirit have their minds set on what the Spirit desires. 6 The mind governed by the flesh is death, but the mind governed by the Spirit is life and peace. 7 The mind governed by the flesh is hostile to God; it does not submit to God's law, nor can it do so. [8] Those who are in the realm of the flesh cannot please God.

[9] You, however, are not in the realm of the flesh but are in the realm of the Spirit, if indeed the Spirit of God lives in you. And if anyone does not have the Spirit of Christ, they do not belong to Christ. [10] But if Christ is in you, then even though your body is subject to death because of sin, the Spirit gives life[d] because of righteousness. [11] And if the Spirit of him who raised Jesus from the dead is living in you, he who raised Christ from the dead will also give life to your mortal bodies because of[e] his Spirit who lives in you.

[12] Therefore, brothers and sisters, we have an obligation—but it is not to the flesh, to live according to it. [13] For if you live according to the flesh, you will die; but if by the Spirit you put to death the misdeeds of the body, you will live.

[14] For those who are led by the Spirit of God are the children of God. [15] The Spirit you received does not make you slaves, so that you live in fear again; rather, the Spirit you received brought about your adoption to sonship.[f] And by him we cry, "Abba,[g] Father." [16] The Spirit himself testifies with our spirit that we are God's children. [17] Now if we are children, then we are heirs—heirs of God and co-heirs with Christ, if indeed we share in his sufferings in order that we may also share in his glory.

Titus 3:4-6

[4] But when the kindness and love of God our Savior appeared, [5] he saved us, not because of righteous things we had done, but because of his mercy. He saved us through the washing of rebirth and renewal by the Holy Spirit, [6] whom he poured out on us generously through Jesus Christ our Savior,

Galatians 5:22-25

[22] But the fruit of the Spirit is love, joy, peace, forbearance, kindness, goodness, faithfulness, [23] gentleness and self-control. Against such things there is no law. [24] Those who belong to Christ Jesus have crucified the flesh with its passions and desires. [25] Since we live by the Spirit, let us keep in step with the Spirit.

In Paul's teachings, likewise, the Spirit then should be described as the initiator and mediator of all that God wishes to give us, in Christ.

Why if all the above is true has the subject of the Holy Spirit been the source of such discord within the life of the Church? Why have Christians 'fallen out' of communion with each other over this subject and why in particular have these divisions been at their worst within the more charismatically inclined Churches?

I would like to suggest two reasons based on my own personal experience over the past 40 years or so.

The First reason: Pentecostalism and the theology of the 'Second Blessing'

The Pentecostal Church believe in something they call the second blessing, a view that has also 'seeped' its way into many other 'Charismatic orientated' churches and movements over the past 40 years. I have come across this 'theology' in one form or another in practically all the Charismatic Churches and movements that I have experienced.

This view states that every Christian must receive a 'second spiritual blessing' or 'Baptism of the Spirit' after their conversion through which God (sort of) 'completes' their conversion and through which he gives them the gifts of his Spirit including the gift of tongues. If you haven't received this experience and the gift of tongues, then you are effectively not in receipt of all that you should be from God and furthermore this is very often regarded as being your fault in some way. You see the obvious division this must cause immediately.

The main problem with this whole view is that it is basically not a theology that I have ever found taught in the N/T! There is no theology of 'The Second blessing.' Anywhere! The few references which Pentecostalism and its followers have used to try to justify such a belief, normally a misguided understanding of Pentecost itself and the conversion of Cornelius's household in Acts chapter 10, blatantly do not mean what they say they do.

Pentecost was clearly, as it says in the text, the fulfilment of the prophecy of Joel, the time when God sent his Spirit back into the lives of his people.

Peter Addresses the Crowd: Acts 2 vs 14 – 21.

14 Then Peter stood up with the Eleven, raised his voice and addressed the crowd: "Fellow Jews and all of you who live in Jerusalem, let me explain this to you; listen carefully to what I say. 15 These people are not drunk, as you suppose. It's only nine in the morning! [16] *No, this is what was spoken by the prophet Joel:*

[17] *"'In the last days, God says, I will pour out my Spirit on all people. Your sons and daughters will prophesy, your young men will see visions, your old men will dream dreams.* [18] *Even on my servants, both men and women, I will pour out my Spirit in those days, and they will prophesy.* [19] *I will show wonders in the heavens above and signs on the earth below, blood and fire and billows of smoke.* [20] *The sun will be turned to darkness and the moon to blood before the coming of the great and glorious day of the Lord.* [21] *And everyone who calls on the name of the Lord will be saved.'"*

Clearly in the above text, Pentecost was the day when God decided to re-ignite his relationship with his people (now his Church in Christ) and in a new and dynamic way. Whereas in the days of the Old Testament God spoke to his people through the prophets, kings and other chosen individuals, in these 'last days' he pours out his presence on everyone initiating a completely new situation. This new situation is one where all who discover faith in Jesus become indwelt with his presence and receive all the benefits which come with adoption, as his children and membership of his new Kingdom.

Acts 10 (our second most misrepresented passage) clearly describes the conversion of Cornelius and his family to the Christian Faith having only previously received the Baptism of John. Their reception of the Holy Spirit was as a result of their conversion. This event would far better be described as the 'Birth of the Gentile Church'. Neither have anything to do with a 'post conversion' second blessing of the Holy Spirit!

Acts 10

Cornelius Calls for Peter

10 At Caesarea there was a man named Cornelius, a centurion in what was known as the Italian Regiment. [2] *He and all his family were devout and God-fearing; he gave generously to those in need and prayed to God regularly.* [3] *One day at about three in the afternoon he had a vision. He distinctly saw an angel of God, who came to him and said, "Cornelius!"*

[4] *Cornelius stared at him in fear. "What is it, Lord?" he asked.*

The angel answered, "Your prayers and gifts to the poor have come up as a memorial offering before God. ⁵ Now send men to Joppa to bring back a man named Simon who is called Peter. ⁶ He is staying with Simon the tanner, whose house is by the sea."

⁷ When the angel who spoke to him had gone, Cornelius called two of his servants and a devout soldier who was one of his attendants. ⁸ He told them everything that had happened and sent them to Joppa.

Peter's Vision

⁹ About noon the following day as they were on their journey and approaching the city, Peter went up on the roof to pray. ¹⁰ He became hungry and wanted something to eat, and while the meal was being prepared, he fell into a trance. ¹¹ He saw heaven opened and something like a large sheet being let down to earth by its four corners. ¹² It contained all kinds of four-footed animals, as well as reptiles and birds. ¹³ Then a voice told him, "Get up, Peter. Kill and eat."

¹⁴ "Surely not, Lord!" Peter replied. "I have never eaten anything impure or unclean."

¹⁵ The voice spoke to him a second time, "Do not call anything impure that God has made clean."

¹⁶ This happened three times, and immediately the sheet was taken back to heaven.

¹⁷ While Peter was wondering about the meaning of the vision, the men sent by Cornelius found out where Simon's house was and stopped at the gate. ¹⁸ They called out, asking if Simon who was known as Peter was staying there.

¹⁹ While Peter was still thinking about the vision, the Spirit said to him, "Simon, three[a] men are looking for you. ²⁰ So get up and go downstairs. Do not hesitate to go with them, for I have sent them."

²¹ Peter went down and said to the men, "I'm the one you're looking for. Why have you come?"

²² The men replied, "We have come from Cornelius the centurion. He is a righteous and God-fearing man, who is respected by all the Jewish people. A

holy angel told him to ask you to come to his house so that he could hear what you have to say." 23 Then Peter invited the men into the house to be his guests.

Peter at Cornelius's House

The next day Peter started out with them, and some of the believers from Joppa went along. 24 The following day he arrived in Caesarea. Cornelius was expecting them and had called together his relatives and close friends. 25As Peter entered the house, Cornelius met him and fell at his feet in reverence. 26But Peter made him get up. "Stand up," he said, "I am only a man myself."

27 While talking with him, Peter went inside and found a large gathering of people. 28He said to them: "You are well aware that it is against our law for a Jew to associate with or visit a Gentile. But God has shown me that I should not call anyone impure or unclean. 29So when I was sent for, I came without raising any objection. May I ask why you sent for me?"

30 Cornelius answered: "Three days ago I was in my house praying at this hour, at three in the afternoon. Suddenly a man in shining clothes stood before me 31 and said, 'Cornelius, God has heard your prayer and remembered your gifts to the poor. 32Send to Joppa for Simon who is called Peter. He is a guest in the home of Simon the tanner, who lives by the sea.' 33So I sent for you immediately, and it was good of you to come. Now we are all here in the presence of God to listen to everything the Lord has commanded you to tell us."

34 Then Peter began to speak: "I now realize how true it is that God does not show favoritism 35but accepts from every nation the one who fears him and does what is right. 36You know the message God sent to the people of Israel, announcing the good news of peace through Jesus Christ, who is Lord of all. 37You know what has happened throughout the province of Judea, beginning in Galilee after the baptism that John preached— 38how God anointed Jesus of Nazareth with the Holy Spirit and power, and how he went around doing good and healing all who were under the power of the devil, because God was with him.

39 "We are witnesses of everything he did in the country of the Jews and in Jerusalem. They killed him by hanging him on a cross, 40 but God raised him from the dead on the third day and caused him to be seen. 41 He was not seen by all the people, but by witnesses whom God had already chosen—by us who ate and drank with him after he rose from the dead. 42 He commanded us to preach to the people and to testify that he is the one whom God appointed as judge of the living and the dead. 43 All the prophets testify about him that everyone who believes in him receives forgiveness of sins through his name."

44 While Peter was still speaking these words, the Holy Spirit came on all who heard the message. 45 The circumcised believers who had come with Peter were astonished that the gift of the Holy Spirit had been poured out even on Gentiles. 46 For they heard them speaking in tongues[b] and praising God.

Then Peter said, 47 "Surely no one can stand in the way of their being baptized with water. They have received the Holy Spirit just as we have." 48So he ordered that they be baptized in the name of Jesus Christ. Then they asked Peter to stay with them for a few days.

This was clearly the very first time that Cornelius and his household had heard and responded to the full Gospel message. The point of this story seems clear, Peter, the head of the Jerusalem (Jewish only Church), is taken by God to Cornelius's home in order for God to show Peter the new inclusivity of the kingdom of God in Christ. Prior to this Peter and the first disciples believed that salvation through Christ was for the benefit of Israel only. They were the chosen people of God Jesus was their Messiah; they were the place where God would rule in his new Kingdom in Christ; they had, up until this moment no conception of the breadth of God's salvation in Jesus; the boundaries that would now be broken down and the extent to which the grace of God would now spread. In Christ, the second Adam, God was re-uniting the whole of his creation with himself, restoring everything that had been lost to him through the Fall of the first Adam.

Nothing, as I have already said, to do with a theology of a 'second, post conversion blessing' of the Holy Spirit which initiates or completes one's conversion to faith in Christ.

One might also clearly suggest that if there was such a need for all Christians to have this 'second blessing', if it really was as essential to the Christian life as some Charismatics' suggest, then it would be present as a major piece of teaching, certainly within the book of Acts and without any doubt in Paul's teachings as well.

This is another example of 'folk Christianity' at its best. Someone, just basically, made this up one day in an attempt to understand the time of revival, out of which Pentecostalism grew years ago and it just stuck.

The second reason for division: The belief that one has come to 'own or possess' the ministry / gifts of the Spirit.

I have consistently seen within the life of Charismatic Churches a tendency to personalise and take 'personal ownership' of the ministries of the Spirit. A practice which is fuelled by, and which in turn leads to, MASSIVE 'personal script satisfaction' (remember the script stuff earlier).

Deep down inside all of us there is an almost inescapable love of power. We all love to feel that we are the most important person around, the 'special one', indispensable, needed, the most blessed! Likewise, many of us also like to believe that our church is the 'best', the most spiritual. Almost without fail Charismatics (unless very careful) in the end, tend to fall foul of this temptation towards pride-filled 'self-delusion.'

In fact, in every Charismatic Church with which I have ever been involved this has tended to happen to some extent or other and nearly always to those who are either in leadership or who have come to be considered to be the most 'blessed' by God.

In some cases, I have even experienced whole sections of the worshipping community literally 'glow' with this sense of superior self-righteousness, convinced as they are that their Church has it right, that they have discovered the true 'Gospel of the Spirit' and are supremely blessed by God because of it. Feeling also blessed of course far more than I and others have been! The root of this 'Pharisaic self-righteousness' expresses itself invariably within, and because of, this belief in their 'ownership' or 'possession of the Gifts of the Spirit. I have also regularly experienced this same sense of self-righteousness amongst many conservative Evangelicals who also believe that they are uniquely right in their understanding of the gospel message and uniquely *the owners or possessors or holders* of the 'all truth' that Jesus spoke about in John 14.

When this phenomenon starts to manifest itself in Charismatic circles the leaders of, and the worshiping community start, saying things like "I *'have been given'* the gift of healing" or "God has *given him* this Gift' or that "God has *'given us'* as a Church, the ministry of this or that". In saying this the particular 'Gift of the Spirit' or 'Spiritual ministry' referred to, becomes subconsciously, at least, seen as something almost separate from the Spirit himself. Furthermore, as something *owned by* or *given to* the specific individual or congregation as their personal *gift or possession*. Like Gollum's ring of Power, in the 'Lord of the rings' trilogy – the spiritual gift or ministry of God's Spirit becomes their own jealously guarded badge of power… it becomes… "***My Precious***"

Time after time I have heard Charismatics speak of the ministries of the Spirit in this way. "David has the gift of healing," praise God! Well, aren't I special now, ohhhh I like that! Soon I am holding special prayer days just for people to come to ME to be prayed for. I am now essential, special and FULL OF MY OWN SELF IMPORTANCE because I OWN a gift of the Spirit! My 'life scripts' of insecurity, of having not had enough love as a child, of my need for recognition and importance etc just love all this. **Big mistake**: Pride, arrogance and division here we come!

On one particular occasion, for example, I was at home in the Vicarage in West Hampstead when I received a phone call from a home group leader of a very large London based Charismatic Church of England Church, she very kindly and somewhat patronisingly, informed me that as part of their ministry, all their members who lived in my Parish were going to visit my Church; stand outside my Church and pray for revival within my Church! She then asked if there was anything in particular that I would like them to pray for. None too impressed, I kindly let her know that we actually already prayed for renewal every week in our own Church and that I was actually quite sure that God listened to us just as much as he did them. I suggested that if they really wanted to pray for us then they should actually pray that God would put it in the hearts of all the Christians who currently lived in my Parish, and yet attend her Church in central London to change their minds and seek to serve God in their own local Parish! Her response was less than positive.

Now, of course, the N/T does indeed talk of the Church exhibiting these signs and wonders and refers to them indeed as 'gifts' but what we must always remember is that these are gifts given for the benefit of the whole church. What is *REALLY* going on, when these gifts begin to manifest themselves within the life of the Church, is, not that God is singling out anyone or any Church congregation to have more holiness and power than others, but rather, that the Spirit, in spite of us, is by God's sheer grace ministering through us for the benefit of his Church. God is not taking a particular bit of the Spirit and giving it to us as our own personal possession. He is working through us; it is he that accomplishes everything, we are simply the clay pots. As soon as we start to consider the Gifts of the Spirit as 'things' which God gives to us we lose perspective completely and fall into the very real danger of developing attitudes and behaviour based on pride, greed, ambition, self-promotion and power.

Finally: we should, mention briefly, to close this section those at the other end of the spectrum who believe that the age of miracles ended with the age of the Apostles! I have never understood why this should be the case, especially, because as I have argued above, the whole point of the coming of the Spirit seems to contradict this suggestion completely. Furthermore, there is no evidence of this being taught within the pages of the N/T and finally, it defies the experience of millions of Christians both today and throughout the ages of the Church.

'The Spirit will lead you into all truth'

One question that we haven't yet tackled is how we might understand what Jesus meant when he told the disciples in John chapter 14 vs 25 that the Spirit would lead them into understanding 'All Truth'. It is a question which I confess I never really took much notice of before but having given it some thought, it seems to me that the best answer I can suggest is based around how we understand the role of the Spirit in the *creation* of the New Testament.

It seems clear from what we have said so far that the Holy Spirit's coming at Pentecost initiated a whole new process of revelation which led the disciples and the early Church into an ever-deepening comprehension of what God had truly done for them and for the world in Christ. This in turn, quite naturally led to the composition of the writings of the N.T. through which this continual and divinely inspired revelation was recorded and taught. This is, of course, why we as the Church consider Scripture to be 'uniquely inspired'. It is the end result of this 'Spiritual revealing' of God's plan and purpose in Christ to the Disciples.

Holy Scripture, then is the result of a divinely inspired co-operation between the human writers and the revelations given to them through the presence and revealing guidance of the Holy Spirit. It is the 'All truth' that Jesus spoke of his gift to us.

Chapter 10

The Trinity

Well, I do have to say that this is a bit of a tricky one. I thought I would start with a few of the 'given's.

In Christian theology, the nature of God is believed to consist of three distinct 'persons', namely, the Father, the Son and the Holy Spirit.

These three 'Persons' are believed to be equal in nature and exist in such a perfect unity / communion / relationship that the Christian faith remains completely monotheistic in nature. There is only one God.

The Christian faith does not believe that there are in some way three Gods who all live together in the same place sharing the odd cuppa over their management of the universe. There is one God, and he has three persons. OK? I am already confused!

How this is explained of course is a different matter. Some suggest that there is a difference but this is a difference in 'space and form' as opposed to 'nature'. So (silly example time) you could have a bucket of pure water, take some out and freeze it, take some out and boil it, at one point in the process you would have 3 different things all however essentially made up of exactly the same components: ice, water, steam all H2O from the same source. In God then, there is God (the source or bucket of water). Jesus (same in nature but a different expression of God; the ice) and the Holy Spirit (same again in nature as the source but different again; the Steam) So all three persons are the same in nature, inextricably linked in both nature and origin, yet still also different. Now, of course, this doesn't tell us 'who God is' but it gives a picture which is perhaps not completely un-helpful? I leave that to you.

Another idea comes from the concept of 'relationship', that is, God's own *internal relationship*.

In this idea, which I first read in Louis Berkhoff's Systematic Theology years ago, God is considered by nature to be 'tri-personal', as opposed to humans who (normally) by nature are uni-personal (have a single personality). This 'tri-personality' is a necessity of the divine being. God could therefore not exist in any other form: this IS who he IS! God also therefor has a general self-consciousness which incorporates all three persons, as well as each of the three persons having a particular individual self-consciousness, at least that's how I have come to understand it. In this way God is able to 'know himself' in perfection and unity. Without this general self-consciousness God would not be able to be self-contemplating, self-aware and self-communing. If you want to know more then read Berkhoff's book

Personally, I find this idea of 'tri-personality' very helpful in trying to comprehend in some small way what is of course 'The mystery of God's personality', the Trinity.

Finally, what exactly does the Church state about the Trinitarian nature of God:

1. There is in the Divine Being one indivisible essence.
2. In this Divine Being there are three persons, namely, the Father, Son and Holy Spirit.
3. The whole undivided essence of God belongs equally to each of the three persons.
4. These three persons within the Divine Being of God are marked by a certain definite order. The Father first from whom the Son is begotten and the Spirit who proceeds from the Father and the Son.
5. There are certain 'personal attributes' by which the three persons are distinguished.
6. The Church confesses the Trinity to be a mystery beyond the comprehension of man. No surprise there!

There are those of course who do not accept the Trinitarian teaching of the Church and some who suggest that it is not a biblical theology at all.

Some evidence of the Trinity in Scripture:

For the Christian Church, in the main, the Trinity is witnessed to primarily in the revelation of Jesus as the Divine Son who has come from the Father and in the outpouring of the Holy Spirit who proceeds from the Father and the Son.

In the 'great commission' Jesus mentions all three persons "....Baptising them in the name of the Father, Son and Holy Spirit" Matt 28:19 and they are named together in 1 Cor 12:4-6, 2Cor 13:14, and 1 Peter 1:2.

We have also, of course, the passages which witness to the Divinity of Christ and the nature of the Holy Spirit which we have dealt with above.

In conclusion, I would suggest, that there is ample evidence within the scriptures to support the contention that God has revealed himself to mankind in three distinct forms: as Father, Son and Spirit, the trinitarian doctrine of God then develops from this.

Chapter 11

The Sacraments

As I am sure most of you good readers already know, the whole concept of 'Sacrament' has also caused some significant discussions within the history of the Church. In the broadest possible terms, a 'Sacrament' should be described as an activity which conveys the grace of God.

Within the Roman Catholic Church, the Orthodox Church, Anglicanism and in Methodism the concept is linked inextricably to the role of the priesthood. Outside the practice of these denominations Church tradition has tended to weaken or even lose completely the relationship between Sacrament and Ordination.

Within both Roman Catholicism, the Orthodox Church, Methodism and Anglicanism, the Eucharist or Holy Communion is considered to be the most important sacrament, along with Baptism, so we will take this as our 'model'.

In Roman Catholicism the Holy Communion may only be administered by a Priest, it is the same for the Church of England, Orthodox Church and within Methodism. The reason for this is simply because in Roman Catholic theology only the Priest has the ability to instigate the 'changing' of the bread and wine into 'vehicles' of God's Grace. By virtue of a Priest's Ordination the Holy Spirit works through the ministry of the Priest and performs a miracle. Once blessed, the bread and wine changes. They 'transubstantiate' which is a very big word for describing the belief that they become the Body and Blood of Jesus. Whilst in their appearance they 'appear' unchanged, in reality they have become Christ's own flesh and blood. As such they become, when taken, the ultimate communication of the 'Grace of God' into men and women's lives. A sacrament then, in this view, may best be described as an activity administered by a Priest by which the Holy Spirit conveys the grace of God.

This is also the case for such things as Baptism, Confession and Absolution which again within the Catholic tradition (Anglican, Orthodox and Methodist) may only be administered by a Priest by virtue of his or her ordination.

In Church of England practice, of course, as with most things C of E this theology is somewhat less defined and whilst the link between ordination and sacrament is maintained, the means by which Grace may be transmitted to believers seems more fluid. In the case of communion, for example, transubstantiation is not a belief generally held, although most would still believe in a 'real presence' of Christ within the meal however undefined this may be.

Others believe in a view proposed by the theologian John Macquarrie called 'Transignification'. In this view the crux of communion depends on a change in the *significance* of the bread and wine within the belief of the recipient, as a result of the Priest's blessing.

A particularly helpful way of explaining transignification:

Imagine that your child takes a piece of plain white paper. He or she then colours onto this a beautiful heart and writes on it "Mummy (or Daddy) I love you". The child then proudly hands you the drawing, now full of all the love that he or she has for you. In one sense this is still only a piece of paper but in another sense, it really isn't. Now, this paper contains a treasured message. It contains also something of your child's nature imprinted upon it, something of their love, something of their very character. The paper has been transformed into a vehicle of that child's love and this is conveyed to you every time you look at it. Even if you were to look at it years later you would still EXPERIENCE that love. The picture is, therefore, not just a memorial but so much more. It has been 'transignificated', it has become 'sacramental' to you! It now conveys in a very real way the love of your child. In a similar way the Eucharist becomes, through the faith of the church, the actions of the Priest and in a dynamic and spiritual way through the ministry of the Spirit, the vehicle by which, we experience by faith, the Love and Grace of God in Christ. Bread and wine, it may still be, but also so much more.

Personally, I quite like this whole idea because it centres the 'Sacramental significance' in the response, (faith) of the believer and in the activity of God through his Spirit ministering to the faithful believer. This emphasises the idea of 'relationship' as the key to God's impartation of Grace within the whole Eucharistic setting. The sense of any 'real presence' of Christ in the actual elements (the bread and the wine) is, clearly, somewhat diminished but as already stated, my belief is that within the N/T it is the role of the Spirit to replace Christ's presence on earth, that it is the Spirit who continues Christ's ministry in and through the Church. In view of this the idea that it is the Spirit who brings 'Sacrament' seems wholly in concert with this teaching. The ritual of the consecration by the Priest becomes, therefor, the key act which triggers this action of Grace within the believer's heart. As they take the bread and wine they respond to God and the Holy Spirit responds to the faith of the believer.

To extend this theory to the other sacraments of the Church again seems to work extremely well. In confession, for example, it is surely God who has forgiven the sin and it is theologically speaking, the Holy Spirit, surely, who has firstly convicted the sinner of their failure and who likewise conveys to that person the assurance of God's forgiveness once they have confessed. The Priestly role becomes the means by which the relationship between the sinner and God is restored and so on for the other sacraments.

A sacrament here then becomes an act carried out by the believer in faith through which God's Holy Spirit brings grace into that believer's life, the relationship between the believer and God is the key and the priestly role, or the role of a minister for that matter, becomes the 'trigger' for this to happen. He is the one who enables this relationship to be renewed and to flourish.

Despite the fact that I lean strongly towards this understanding, I am unwilling to dismiss other concepts, such as that of Roman Catholicism, because I strongly suspect that to do this would simply limit the ways that God chooses to bring his love into our lives. I am happy with the concept of ordination because I believe firmly that at ordination God bestows upon men and women a unique ministry within the Church, this was without doubt my own experience at my ordination. Coming as I did from a non-conformist background, prior to my call into the C of E, it was not an experience I was expecting. However, after that day, I really felt that God had given me something new.

I am quite sure that ultimately it is the Holy Spirit who consecrates and who initiates and completes the whole sacramental process. I am quite sure that it is he who is the conveyer of all grace and that he is free to do this in a variety of ways both through and independently of priesthood.

Furthermore, in my opinion, all of the kingdom's blessings are Sacraments, not only the named ones but also prayer, the laying on of hands, forgiveness, love, kindness etc, ALL, if done 'in Christ' are, by Gods Spirit conveyers of grace, both from God to us and as his body the Church from whom rivers of living water flow, from us to each other. Perhaps, ultimately, we should accept that as the Church collective we are all potentially conduits of grace by the ministry of the Spirit? As we deal in miracles and mystery it might be best then to not limit God at all but rather embrace all the possibilities.

Chapter 12

Worship

Throughout my Christian life, I have found that the question of what entails 'proper worship' to be a hotly debated issue. For some, form, liturgy and sacrament are the corner stones, while for others, what we might call 'fluidity and freedom of expression' have been extolled as the only true way to approach the throne of grace and there are, of course, numerous variations within these two main themes.

In addition to these 'preferences' the practice of worship is often also further complicated by our own personal motivations. This can be because of pride, by our inherited beliefs in what is 'correct' or 'proper' and more recently, by the infatuation with the 'promotion of the self' encouraged by the development of the so called 'celebrity culture'. This has spawned in its wake such self-promoting mediums as 'Reality T.V.', 'Big Brother', 'Face book', 'twitter' and the like which cater for, a now quite prevalent need in so many, to achieve their '15 minutes of fame'. For reasons, perhaps, of our own innate insecurity and negative life scripts, countless numbers of ordinary people need now to feel that they are in the spotlight in some way, often advertising the most unimportant aspects of their lives in the hope that they are somehow interesting to others. This satisfies, it seems, some need within themselves to feel special, important, famous and valued. The users of such social media sites seek their own followers, virtual friends, most of whom they have never even met. All of this, to me, just seems a little sad.

In relation to Worship, however, to stick to our theme, this same culture of 'self-promotion' can affect our attitudes, our emotions and often our motivations in worship, as they bleed into our egos and insecurities.

I was standing in one of my colleague's church vestibules some years ago while I was a Priest at my first Church St Cuthbert's West Hampstead, when I saw what was, I suspect, one of the finest acts of just this sort of self deception.

The Church in question shall of course remain nameless, but suffice to say, it is one of the typically successful large Charismatic Anglican Churches based in London.

I had just been to a Deanery Synod meeting. In the room next to us a group of Charismatic Christians had been holding one of those fairly well-known guitar led prayer meetings. As I waited in the said Foyer, I looked into the room from which the said musical was coming, to see a lady looking straight at me. She had a sort of pained smile on her face and was running on the spot in time to the music. On catching my eye, she forced a greater smile (while still running on the spot) as if to convince me that she was 'In the Spirit' in some way and actually worshiping God. My first and only thought was that she must be suffering quite badly from some sort of mental health issue and as the song had been going for at least 30 minutes, extremely tired. She looked fairly elderly, at least too old to be running endlessly on the spot. It did cross my mind that she might have a heart attack and die............ why doesn't she stop? I mused as the pained and brave smile on her face continued.

Everyone else in that room probably believed that she was worshipping God, but I felt quite convinced she wasn't. She seemed rather to be 'playing along' or 'fitting in' she was bowing to peer pressure, doing that which she thought she had too in order to be accepted as 'Kosher' and, for some and in many different traditions, this is sadly the basic quality of what we mistakenly call, our offering of worship. We play along with the crowd and we convince ourselves whilst doing this, that we are worshipping in Spirit and in Truth. We want to be seen as one who has got it right and receive in doing this our 15 mins of positive reinforcement or if you like, 'fame'. Often this desire for recognition, this needing to be accepted, is perhaps one of the greatest barriers I have ever experienced to true worship.

In another example from the other end of the traditional spectrum, when I was studying for the Anglican Priesthood, I attended a Good Friday service in my College Chapel. I personally can't say I enjoyed College services much but I tried each time to approach the various aspects with sincerity and prayer.

On this occasion, however, it was announced that at the end of the service there would be an opportunity for people to spend time meditating on Christ's death at the foot of the rather large Cross situated at the front of the Church as I suppose one might expect on Good Friday. I stayed for a while, frankly, to show willing. As I did, however, some of the students decided that praying was simply not enough so they got up and began to lay face down on the concrete floor. This I have to say I found immediately rather bizarre. Then as time passed some began to make a sort of moaning noise, at which point others started to wail, and others cry. The more each one did, so another's intensified until in order to bring to an end this competition of self flagellation I felt as if the winner was just going to have to die as well! When each had finished this apparently Spirit filled mortification at the Cross they would get up, smile, chat and off they would go no doubt supremely satisfied that they had been one of the more reverent of our group! Needless to say, I just left to get some dinner. How this attempt at self-gratification and celebrity could ever be considered to be true worship escapes me entirely.

So, what is worship?

Well in this particular context, it is I would suggest nothing more or less than the sincere veneration and contemplation of God in Christ brought about through the enabling presence of the Holy Spirit in our lives, however we choose to express it. The form doesn't matter. It is only the sincerity with which it is carried out and the relationship to God in the Spirit which prompts the response. There is also, I would suggest, no better worship style but only that which enables believers to respond and to commune with God and this can be achieved by ritual, liturgy, song, meditation, by word or in silence. The only important factors are the presence of God by his Spirit and our deliberate and sincere quest to seek to respond to God's Love and to find our God in penitence, gratitude and faith.

It is hugely important, of course, to remember that biblically speaking, true spiritual worship as the Apostle Paul reminds us in Romans chapter 12, has actually little to do with how we express ourselves in public worship but is rather categorised as an expression of our whole lives lived within the knowledge and presence of God in Christ.

*'Therefore, I urge you, brothers and sisters, in view of God's mercy, to offer your bodies as a **living sacrifice**, holy and pleasing to God—this is your true and proper worship. Do not conform to the pattern of this world but be transformed by the renewing of your mind. Then you will be able to test and approve what God's will is—his good, pleasing and perfect will."* We will deal with the full meaning of this text now in our next chapter.

Chapter 13

Living Sacrifices

In the next couple of chapters I would like to look a little at what Christians call discipleship. I will do this, firstly, through the picture of 'Sacrifice' and then spend some time thinking about the tensions that exist between our desire to follow Christ and the potentially distracting influences of the world around us.

A Living Sacrifice; Romans Chapter 12

'Therefore, I urge you, brothers and sisters, in view of God's mercy, to offer your bodies as a living sacrifice, holy and pleasing to God—this is your true and proper worship. [2] Do not conform to the pattern of this world, but be transformed by the renewing of your mind. Then you will be able to test and approve what God's will is—his good, pleasing and perfect will.'

Having touched on the need for Christians to live 'good and holy lives' and without confusing this with any belief that to do so in any way acts as a CONDITION of God's grace or of a means of securing 'more' grace, I thought it might be helpful for us to look a little at what Paul means when he talks about discipleship. A concept which is described in the text above in terms of 'a living sacrifice'.

The whole idea of ritual sacrifice was of course embedded within Jewish religious practice and these practices fed of course, directly into the N/T theology of Christ's own death on the cross which was and is seen in Christian thought to be the ultimate blood sacrifice which takes away completely the sin of the world.

To offer oneself to God as a 'living sacrifice', as the Apostle Paul here suggests, implies naturally, mirroring the example of Christ's sacrifice on the cross, a totality of giving.

We give to God our hopes and our dreams, our private lives, our secrets, our lives at home, our lives at work, our possible futures and the world of our past. Nothing is held back. There are no bits then in this analogy kept just for us. Everything we are is offered to God on the altar of our faith.

But how can we do this when so much of what we are is not particularly holy at all? We may, for example, have elements within our past and present that we would not share even with our closest friends. How can we share them then with God?

In regard to our futures, are we willing to take the chance that what **we** want to achieve might not be what God wants for us? Furthermore, the way that we want to live our lives now, may not be the way that God would have us live. It is an inescapable fact that the content of our lives might be challenged by the principles of our faith. Will we submit those areas to change? Will we rise to this challenge? We may well accept, of course, that we are 'completely saved' by virtue of our choice of faith and that our commitment to holy living doesn't come as a 'condition' of God's grace. Even so, there is no doubt, that such a commitment to sacrifice as encouraged here within the New Testament is still exceptionally challenging.

One issue which further complicates this 'sacrificial' response to Christ is our ability to psychologically compartmentalise our lives. All of us, I suspect to one extent or another, end up splitting our lives into the good bits and the bad hoping that on balance, the bad bits will be outweighed or even justified by the good in some way. For example: the youth leader who spends his life helping the most troubled of teenagers has a family, but also, on the side, visits a prostitute. The hard-working family man who has an addiction to gambling; the wife who seeks out comfort from another because at home she feels lonely; or the sexual fantasies that we all indulge at times and so on. Most people have their secrets and Christians are no different. Many people indeed hide parts of their lives away from their friends, their family and in regard to our subject here, many religious people try to hide them from God as well. It is just this sort of compartmentalization of religion and life that Paul is arguing against here in our passage. So, how can we offer **all that we are** to God when so much of what we are, in reality, is so far from acceptable? How can we truly be a living sacrifice? And the simple answer is that we can because of Christ, because of his sin offering death on the cross at Calvary. This is the miracle of the Gospel. We can, because we have already been made 'perfect in Gods eye's' by this faith, he accepts us, sin and all. We can offer EVERYTHING that we are because in Christ we are forgiven and as such we can offer ourselves without fear of condemnation and even discover, in that offering, the possibility of being transformed. We have the opportunity in offering all this rubbish to

God, to be re-created, made new, born again throughout **all** the different parts or compartments of our being.

We also, of course, tend to see 'conversion' as a one-off event when perhaps it would be far better to see 'conversion' as a process by which we enter into in partnership with God. Here we discover his forgiveness and grace, a forgiveness and grace which continues for the rest of our lives.

As the Apostle puts it: "Do not be conformed to this world, but be *transformed* (in the continuous tense) by the renewal of your mind,"

We offer all that we are to God so that we can be sanctified, re-directed, and changed from the inside out, transformed by the power of God's Spirit who now lives within us. Being a failure, being a sinner, making mistakes, being on the <u>road towards</u> becoming a good Christian is nothing to be ashamed of. It is, in fact, the truth of who we are, we need to accept that. As the Apostle says in vs 3 of our text.

3 For by the grace given me I say to every one of you: Do not think of yourself more highly than you ought, but rather think of yourself with sober judgment, in accordance with the faith God has distributed to each of you.

God doesn't expect us to be any more than we are! What he expects is for us to give who we are to him completely so that he can turn us into the people we have always wanted to be – 'be transformed by the renewing of your mind'.

Furthermore, it is also very important to realise that having a successful faith doesn't mean that we all end up as clones of some perfect Christian model. This is a typical mistake often made by the evangelicals and, in particular, the more charismatic of us. It's a bit like the Jehovah Witnesses isn't it? Have you noticed that when they come to your door all the men look the same; short cropped hair, usually clean shaven and in identical suits. It's as if they have been secretly bred in some God ordained birth chamber in the U.S.A. as part of some secret religious end time experiment to produce the perfect looking Christian. The implication of their conformity is designed to convince us that only they, and people just like them, will be saved. Only they will be met at the rapture of God. This is of course nonsense. Being the holy people of God doesn't mean uniformity. The human condition makes this simply impossible, as we have already said. In fact, the Bible is quite clear that our diversity is also built into the equation because God wants every part of us and all of us. He wants all of our talents, our characters, our personalities and intends to use each of us to the best of OUR abilities, rather than seek to turn us all into some cloned human representation of a divine perfect person. God accepts us in the diversity of who we are and seeks to capitalise on these differences even within his new Kingdom.

1 Corinthians chapter 12.

⁴ There are different kinds of gifts, but the same Spirit distributes them. ⁵ There are different kinds of service, but the same Lord. ⁶ There are different kinds of working, but in all of them and in everyone it is the same God at work.

⁷ Now to each one the manifestation of the Spirit is given for the common good. ⁸

The call is then for us to offer to God 'who we are, and all that we are' and God will respond and use who we are and our individual personalities and talents to serve in his Kingdom. And of course, we must always remember that rather than God blessing those of us who THINK we are successful and strong God rather blesses us all when we are fully able to acknowledge our weakness and failure, *"Gods strength is made perfect in our weakness".*

In summary, then, let us seek to offer the whole of ourselves to God as living sacrifices so that he may transform us into his people and through his Church united show his grace to the world.

Overcoming the World:

For part 2 of this discussion on discipleship I have picked two further passages for us to ponder, one from Paul's teachings and the other from the Gospels.
Romans 12:9-21

Love in action.

⁹ Love must be sincere. Hate what is evil; cling to what is good. ¹⁰ Be devoted to one another in love. Honour one another above yourselves. ¹¹ Never be lacking in zeal, but keep your spiritual fervour, serving the Lord. ¹² Be joyful in hope, patient in affliction, faithful in prayer. ¹³ Share with the Lord's people who are in need. Practice hospitality.

¹⁴ Bless those who persecute you; bless and do not curse. ¹⁵ Rejoice with those who rejoice; mourn with those who mourn. ¹⁶ Live in harmony with one another. Do not be proud, but be willing to associate with people of low position. Do not be conceited.

[17] Do not repay anyone evil for evil. Be careful to do what is right in the eyes of everyone. [18] If it is possible, as far as it depends on you, live at peace with everyone. [19] Do not take revenge, my dear friends, but leave room for God's wrath, for it is written: "It is mine to avenge; I will repay," says the Lord. [20] On the contrary:

"If your enemy is hungry, feed him; if he is thirsty, give him something to drink. In doing this, you will heap burning coals on his head."

[21] Do not be overcome by evil, but overcome evil with good.

The Yeast of the Pharisees and Sadducees: Matthew 16 vs 5 - 12

[5] When they went across the lake, the disciples forgot to take bread. [6] "Be careful," Jesus said to them. "Be on your guard against the yeast of the Pharisees and Sadducees." ....[11] How is it you don't understand that I was not talking to you about bread? But be on your guard against the yeast of the Pharisees and Sadducees." [12] Then they understood that he was not telling them to guard against the yeast used in bread, but against the teaching of the Pharisees and Sadducees."

As we travel along our journey of life it is impossible, I am sure you will agree, not to be affected, moulded and changed by the world around us. We are bombarded from the day we are born with all types of influences both for good and bad which all converge together like a symphony of music around us to make us who we are. This carries on throughout our lives whether we like it or not. Some psychologists say that each of us is, in fact, in constant change and that the person we are today will always differ from the person we will become tomorrow. Sometimes these changes are so small that we wouldn't notice and sometimes, if we are exposed to more significant events and influences, they can be quite obvious and dramatic. In addition to this there is always the sort of 'drip drip' effect from our life experiences that change us constantly over a longer period of time.

I, for example, as you all know by now, was a police officer for 30 years and it is fair to say that 30 years of dealing almost everyday with the more difficult members of our society has influenced who I am and effected changes in me which at times I have not been so happy with. There are times when the influence of life as a police officer has made me quite intolerant of certain people. It has caused me to hold opinions which are perhaps not those which I would want to hold in the cold light of day. Being a police officer can tend, if you are not careful, to cause you to de-humanize certain groups and it can make you quite cynical about people in general.

It can also, no doubt of course, provide you with an enormous amount of common sense, life experience, practical skills and knowledge. Over-all the psychological consequences of life as a Police Officer is a mixed bag and to some extent the negative aspects are part of the cost you become willing to pay in the service of your community.

The same can be said, of course, for many professions and as I have said, none of us are ever free from the influences of life and the world around us. All of us have relationships which affect us. All of us can experience crime, suffering, love, hate, happiness, tragedy, Joy, hope, good jobs, bad jobs, the news and so on. We are then as individuals a collection of what life has made us.

Why are we talking about this?

In the readings above from Romans and from the Gospel of Matthew both the Apostle Paul and our Lord talk about the sort of influences and characteristics that should dominate our lives, and by definition of course, those which we should try to ignore, avoid, fight against and change.

In the Romans reading Paul continues on from our previous 'Living Sacrifice' theme and talks about our need to be transformed through the influence of Gods Spirit within our lives, setting out what the results of this new Spiritual influence on our lives should be.

Love in Action - Romans 12

⁹Love must be sincere. Hate what is evil; cling to what is good. ¹⁰Be devoted to one another in love. Honour one another above yourselves. ¹¹Never be lacking in zeal, but keep your spiritual fervour, serving the Lord. ¹²Be joyful in hope, patient in affliction, faithful in prayer. ¹³Share with the Lord's people who are in need. Practice hospitality.

¹⁴Bless those who persecute you; bless and do not curse. ¹⁵Rejoice with those who rejoice; mourn with those who mourn. ¹⁶Live in harmony with one another. Do not be proud, but be willing to associate with people of low position Do not be conceited.

¹⁷Do not repay anyone evil for evil. Be careful to do what is right in the eyes of everyone. ¹⁸If it is possible, as far as it depends on you, live at peace with everyone. ¹⁹Do not take revenge, my dear friends, but leave room for God's wrath, for it is written: "It is mine to avenge; I will repay,"[d] says the Lord. ²⁰On the contrary:

"If your enemy is hungry, feed him; if he is thirsty, give him something to drink. In doing this, you will heap burning coals on his head."

²¹Do not be overcome by evil, but overcome evil with good.

The key text, for our current subject, is found in the very last line.

Verse 21 Do not be overcome by evil but overcome evil with good."

It's clear that Paul recognises here the way, as we have just said, that we can be and have been moulded by the world. Our offering of ourselves as living sacrifices involves the recognition by us, that without exception and because of these influences, we hold attitudes and opinions which are anti-God. Our natural inclinations are not to embrace the principles of Love. We must change our lives and resist the temptation to continue to be overcome with this evil. We must overcome the evil of this world instead with good, through the counterbalance of our Christian faith.

There is also the danger of succumbing to wider social and political manipulation. In our Gospel reading from Matthew we find Jesus warning his disciples against the influence of the religious leaders of his day "Be on your guard against the yeast of the Pharisees and Sadducees." These religious leaders had become, because of their snobbery and hypocrisy, a powerfully negative influence on the religious society of Jesus's day. Like bad yeast their poisonous, separatist and divisive agendas had spread capriciously through the populous, causing some parts of their society to become a reflection of that propaganda. We likewise experience similar influences daily through our exposure to the social, political and media forces of our own world. These forces quietly mould us until, we find ourselves, if we are not careful, holding opinions which appear to be both rational and true, but which are in fact inaccurate, biased, and even damaging. As with those more personal influences, the Gospel faith calls us to step back and to question, to have a degree of self-awareness, to challenge what we are being told is the accepted norm and to march out of step at times with the popular agenda because the worlds values are very often not the values of Christ.

To suggest that this doesn't or can't happen flies in the face of all the evidence. One only needs to look at Nazi Germany during the Second World War or the other genocides since that have occurred since worldwide. Huge populations have become convinced of the illegitimacy of another group or race purely by the propaganda of their leaders. Take the current rise of right-wing politics across Europe; to the lies which led so many of us to support the war in Iraq; or even to the lies that most recently and which so powerfully influenced the Brexit vote in the UK. We are subject to incredibly powerful influences on every level of our lives, many of which do not reflect the Christian principles of faith and which mould us towards anti-Christian views and behaviour. Paul's words of warning ring as true today as they have ever done. **"Do not be overcome with evil but overcome evil with good"**. Being a reflection of Christ in the world takes constant re-evaluation, self-awareness and an ability to compare society's social, political and moral agendas with the love of God, as revealed in Jesus Christ.

Chapter 14

Justification by Faith

In the next couple of chapter's, we will take a short look at some of the Apostle Paul's teachings starting here with the theology of 'Justification by Faith alone'. This idea is, believe it or not, something that many people find particularly hard to accept, conditioned as we are to see the whole idea of 'Gift' as, in general terms, an act made in response to something that we have already done. After all we don't usually either give or receive gifts from people to whom we 'owe' nothing, even if that 'owing' is a debt of friendship or for that matter receive 'gifts' from people with whom we have no previous positive relations.

As I mentioned in the introduction, when I was 22 or so I attempted and eventually failed to become a Baptist minister. In the course of this journey to slight disaster I was initially given a student placement and spent about a year at the Gillingham Baptist Church in Kent as a student Pastor. Whilst there I took part in the 'Evangelism Explosion' training course; a course designed to train people in sharing the Gospel.

The course started with a diagnostic question - "If you were to die tonight and stand before God and he were to ask you 'Why should I let you into my heaven?' What would you say?' The answer to which determined what you were *trusting in,* in order to be saved, which brings us to the crux of the matter at hand.

Most people when asked this question usually answer in relation to themselves. People think that they will get to heaven and be acceptable to God because, well, they are not too bad. Most people would say something like "well why not" "I am not a bad person, I never killed anyone, I did my best, why shouldn't I get in?" "There's a lot worse than me out there!" and so on.

The problem with this view, which in itself doesn't seem unreasonable on first consideration, is that the idea that any of us, even the best, could ever be good enough to 'earn our way' into heaven stems in reality from two misapprehensions. Firstly, the misapprehension that fundamentally we are good, and secondly from the mistake of believing that our 'comparison web site', if you like, for such a judgment is humanity itself.

We like to think that we are good, but any sense of goodness that we possess is always relative to our chosen community. In the 'go compare.com' comparison web site of humanity we might actually fair quite well but in the 'go compare.com' comparison web site of prison populations, for example, burglars and robbers do quite well because compared to murderers and paedophiles they're pretty good! You see my point, I hope.

The real question then, the one that really matters, is how do we fair in the 'go compare.com' comparison web site of heaven, of Gods standards, of Gods absolute perfection? When we stand within that particular 'comparison web site' how will we do if we are trusting only in our own goodness for salvation?

According to the Apostle Paul not well.

Romans chapter 1

8 'The wrath of God is being revealed from heaven against all the godlessness and wickedness of people, who suppress the truth by their wickedness, 19 since what may be known about God is plain to them, because God has made it plain to them. 20 For since the creation of the world God's invisible qualities—his eternal power and divine nature—have been clearly seen, being understood from what has been made, so that people are without excuse. 21 For although they knew God, they neither glorified him as God nor gave thanks to him.'

The point is quite plain. Humanity is doomed because it has simply failed to worship God as it should and never mind all our other millions of imperfections and sins and in failing to do this we have all become wicked in God's eyes and objects of his wrath and we are without excuse. It isn't a question of doing enough good or trying to repair the damage. Yes, we might end up being good compared to most of the world but there is no comparison between even our best and the goodness which is God. According to Paul we have failed already. If we rely on ourselves there is no hope. This idea is what some theologians describe as the 'total depravity of mankind'. By now, of course, the liberals have burnt this chapter and the humanists are cursing me as one who simply wishes to condemn humanity as if the acceptance of this teaching is in some way a depressing vocation but is it, or is it in fact the only way to true freedom?

To accept our absolute hopelessness before God, you see, is in fact not a condemnation of our souls; it is rather the means by which we realize the joyfulness of God's Grace. To accept our utter desolation is in fact to realise our need of God;

our need of forgiveness; it is to cast all our cares upon him; it is to seek salvation where it truly CAN be found; to hurl ourselves only onto Christ is to discover all that God has to give. It is our arrogance and stupidity that keeps us away and which seals our doom, not any lack of willingness from God. We struggle and struggle to reach up to God. We build our towers of Babel and our Jacob's ladders when what we should really do is just let go.

The truth is that we all need this salvation and it is in recognising this need, in realising that of ourselves we can never reach God that we discover the God who reaches down to us, the God of the Incarnation and the God of the Spirit, the God of our salvation. Jesus came to us in the form of a human being in order to bring us up with him to heaven. Jesus came down to us as a human being in order to be with us within the quagmire of our lives. Jesus came down to us as a human being in order to take us through our darkest times; to minister to us when we are sick, to bring us home when we are lost, to take us through the valley of the shadow of death and then even through death itself.

In truth, the only way that we can discover this wonderful grace is to abandon ourselves and any confidence that we might have in our own abilities, humble ourselves under God's mighty hand so that he can lift us up. That great old, and in places much maligned theology of the Total Depravity of Mankind is in fact the theology which leads us to our salvation, found only when we rely completely on God's tender care and we need to grasp this point before we can get to grips with our topic for this chapter.

The Apostle Paul puts it most succinctly when he says *"It is by grace you have been saved through Faith and this is the gift of God not by works so that none can boast"*.

So, we cannot find Gods salvation through our own abilities and we need faith to appropriate this grace.

Another common misconception around this whole idea of salvation by faith alone is found within Paul's letter to the Galatians:

Galatians 3 New International Version (NIV)

Faith or Works of the Law

3 You foolish Galatians! Who has bewitched you? Before your very eyes Jesus Christ was clearly portrayed as crucified. 2 I would like to learn just one thing from you: Did you receive the Spirit by the works of the law, or by believing what you heard? 3 Are you so foolish? After beginning by means of the Spirit, are you now trying to finish by means of the flesh? 4 Have you experienced so much in vain—if it really was in vain? 5 So again I ask, does God give you his Spirit and work miracles among you by the works of the law, or by your believing what you heard? 6 So also Abraham "believed God, and it was credited to him as righteousness."

Here Paul addresses his readers in relation to a heresy that had infiltrated his Church and which had been brought to his congregations by a group of Jewish Christians who had set out from Jerusalem in a dedicated quest to supersede Paul's ministry. These 'Judaiasers', as Paul calls them, believed that in order to be saved Paul's gentile converts had to, not only embrace faith in Christ, but also adopt the practice of circumcision and certain other aspects of the old Jewish law. As you can see, Paul vehemently disagreed with this. As far as Paul was concerned his new converts needed no 'add-ons' to their faith and in fact to 'add on' anything to their new faith in Christ (in this case aspects of Old Testament Jewish law) actually nullified their faith in the first place.

For us, as Christians today, this same practice of 'adding on' to our faith is likewise a common experience within Churches. Roman Catholics, for example, 'add-on' the sacraments; so, you MUST be baptised / take communion / be confirmed etc in order to be part of God's Church - to be saved.

For many, particularly conservative evangelicals we find that the 'add on's' appear as well, but normally, in a far more subtle way. Evangelicals will say quite clearly that they believe that Salvation is by faith alone but then, and despite this, some will subtlety subvert this message of freedom through their preaching and teaching on such things as forgiveness, holiness and lifestyle. Interestingly this teaching is also and often, accompanied by the same sort of pharisaic self-righteousness I have experienced within the Charismatic movement described above. Holiness, discipleship, and lifestyle then become indirectly, but nevertheless inseparably linked to and 'added on' to faith in the same way as above. Invariably where *others* lifestyles differs from their own perception of the Christian life these Christians salvation is considered to be null and void. At the very least they are considered to be living in rebellion to God and in danger of falling away or out of his grace unless, of course, they repent and become like them!

The Apostle Paul, of course, dealt with these sorts of misconceptions over lifestyle in his letter to the Church in Rome in chapter 14.

Romans 14

The Weak and the Strong

14 Accept the one whose faith is weak, without quarreling over disputable matters. ² One person's faith allows them to eat anything, but another, whose faith is weak, eats only vegetables. ³ The one who eats everything must not treat with contempt the one who does not, and the one who does not eat everything must not judge the one who does, for God has accepted them. ⁴ Who are you to judge someone else's servant? To their own master, servants stand or fall. And they will stand, for the Lord is able to make them stand.

⁵ One person considers one day more sacred than another; another considers every day alike. Each of them should be fully convinced in their own mind. ⁶ Whoever regards one day as special does so to the Lord. Whoever eats meat does so to the Lord, for they give thanks to God; and whoever abstains does so to the Lord and gives thanks to God. ⁷ For none of us lives for ourselves alone, and none of us dies for ourselves alone. ⁸ If we live, we live for the Lord; and if we die, we die for the Lord. So, whether we live or die, we belong to the Lord. ⁹ For this very reason, Christ died and returned to life so that he might be the Lord of both the dead and the living.

¹⁰ You, then, why do you judge your brother or sister? Or why do you treat them with contempt? For we will all stand before God's judgment seat. ¹¹ It is written:

"'As surely as I live,' says the Lord, 'every knee will bow before me; every tongue will acknowledge God.'"

¹² So then, each of us will give an account of ourselves to God.

¹³ Therefore let us stop passing judgment on one another. Instead, make up your mind not to put any stumbling block or obstacle in the way of a brother or sister. ¹⁴ I am convinced, being fully persuaded in the Lord Jesus, that nothing is unclean in itself. But if anyone regards something as unclean, then for that person it is unclean. ¹⁵ If your brother or sister is distressed because of what you eat, you are no longer acting in love. Do not by your eating destroy someone for whom Christ died. ¹⁶ Therefore do not let what you know is good be spoken of as evil. ¹⁷ For the kingdom of God is not a matter of eating and drinking, but of righteousness, peace and joy in the Holy Spirit, ¹⁸ because anyone who serves Christ in this way is pleasing to God and receives human approval.

¹⁹ Let us therefore make every effort to do what leads to peace and to mutual edification. ²⁰ Do not destroy the work of God for the sake of food. All food is clean, but it is wrong for a person to eat anything that causes someone else to stumble. ²¹ It is better not to eat meat or drink wine or to do anything else that will cause your brother or sister to fall.

²² So whatever you believe about these things keep between yourself and God. Blessed is the one who does not condemn himself by what he approves. ²³ But whoever has doubts is condemned if they eat, because their eating is not from faith; and everything that does not come from faith is sin.

Perhaps the most important point to note within this whole passage is the open and honest acknowledgment by Paul of the differences that exist between all of us as Christians. Each of us has a different understanding of what it means to be a faithful Christian. Each of us has different ideas on what makes us holy and each of us has different struggles which we face and have to battle through in our quest to live a better life for God. Each of us have started this race from a different point depending on our background, our upbringing, our inherited genetic make-up, psychological make up and personal life experiences. We cannot then in any realistic way map out a programme of what makes a Christian holy and acceptable to God. As soon as we start to do this, we miss the point of our miraculous salvation in Christ; reject the truth of our salvation by faith alone and start placing 'add ons' to our faith denying the efficacy of the cross altogether and, as the Apostle Paul says, 'nullifying our Faith.'

We must avoid any suggestion, that in order to discover salvation, we HAVE to be holy or that we HAVE to be committed or HAVE to live in a certain way; or that we HAVE to be a heterosexual or if not, celibate. Or HAVE to be penitent or Baptised in the Spirit and so on. All of these, if they are seen even subconsciously as ***necessary*** for salvation to work, become no different than the ideas put forward by the Judaiasers in Galatia. Just like the teaching of the Judaiasers in Galatia they fundamentally tie us up again in chains, lead us to salvation by works and undermine the true teaching of the Gospel.

To re-iterate Paul's teaching:

"We are saved by Grace through FAITH this is NOT FROM OURSELVES but is the gift of God NOT BY WORKS so that none can boast" and by this Paul doesn't mean Faith AND anything else at all…just FAITH!

Now this doesn't mean, of course, that we shouldn't seek to live a life worthy of our calling. That goes, I hope, without saying. Nothing that I have said above is meant to change the fact that, as Christians, we have a duty to live in love for humankind and in the best way we can for God. The difference is found in the motivation for such living. We choose to live for Christ not because we think that by doing so we are *securing our salvation* but because we are grateful for this great *salvation already given* by virtue of our choice of faith in Christ and the difference between these two ideas is enormous.

We are saved only through the sheer grace of God in response to our act of faith in Jesus Christ. We live therefor in gratitude and more importantly in freedom from fear.

Chapter 15

The consequences of Faith

Everything we do and every decision we make has consequences. This is one of the greatest lessons in life that we can learn. Every stone dropped in a pond however big or small gives out ripples that can cross at times even the whole pond. This sounds obvious, of course, and yet how often do we forget this simple truth and forget perhaps also, that the consequences created by our actions and decisions more often than not, reflect the character of the act performed or decision made. If we make bad decisions, then generally bad consequences follow and vice versa.

When we are considering our life choices it is probably a wise practice to consider first what might be the potential results, both for ourselves and also, of course, for others. 'Look before you leap'.

It is, of course, also very important to realise that it is not only what we do which has consequences but what we fail to do as well.

It should therefore be of no surprise to us at all that exactly the same rules apply to the questions of faith.

Many people don't really think this way about faith because faith nowadays within society (and sometimes within the Church as well) is treated as if it is merely an optional extra to life rather than as an imperative. Furthermore, the idea of our acceptance by God is considered by most, at least outside the Church to be a matter of morality rather than religion. What people do with faith then is something of an irrelevance and, needless to say, this is not a view that was shared by Jesus or the writers of the New Testament.

For our Lord and the NT writers, faith was indeed an essential dynamic in how God sees humanity and how he will respond to us as individuals in terms of relationship and eternity.

The NT lists numerous consequences resulting from a decision to accept the Christian faith. Of these I thought we might like to take a little time to consider two.

- Peace with God.

- Access to God.

Firstly, according to the New Testament, when we take the decision to believe in Jesus Christ, we discover peace with God.

Romans chapter 5 vs 1 and 2.

> *'Therefore, since we have been justified through faith, we have **peace with God** through our Lord Jesus Christ, through whom we have gained access by faith into this grace in which we now stand.'*

In general terms, we tend to see 'being at peace' with someone as a situation resulting from our own decision and frame of mind. Under normal circumstances if I have a falling out with someone, I will feel at peace with that person only when I have reached a point of acceptance and / or forgiveness. Before I reach that point, I am angry perhaps or hurt or whatever, but I have no peace. Peace comes then only when I am emotionally ready.

However when the N/T talks of men and women being at peace with God it is describing a very different situation. This idea of 'reconciliation' is not suggesting that the consequence of faith is that we change our relationship with God because we decide to become his friend. It is rather the opposite way round. Faith brings reconciliation because it provides the means through which God finds himself at peace with us and this, in itself, is a far more important dynamic for us to consider. How we see God is far less important than how he sees us. How he sees us is the determining factor for everything that follows, because he is God!

The fundamental point being made here is simply that once we choose to accept Christ by faith our 'state' before God, from that point onwards, never depends on the frailty of our humanity. It is God who determines where we stand in terms of our relationship to him. In regard to the questions of forgiveness and salvation this is very good news because if these situations were to continue to be determined by us, with our varying degrees of human inconsistency, then surely any sense of security within our relationship with God would be lost.

As a response to our faith then, God makes the decision to accept us as his children and places himself at peace with us. We are forgiven, reconciled and loved and because this situation comes as a result of **God's movement and decision** rather than ours. Nothing we do can ever change it.

Secondly the N/T also tells us that in addition to Peace with God a further consequence of our faith is that we have '**access to God.**'

Everywhere we go nowadays we come across the issue of access. If we get on a train or tube we have to swipe a card to get through the barriers At airports we have security checks. When I worked at police stations, I had to swipe in. Locked doors, barriers with security checks have become our everyday experience and access depends on whether we have qualified to pass or paid the price to get in.

In God's kingdom similar rules apply. Access to God, at least the unique access that faith in Christ provides, requires us also to be qualified. The difference here, of course, is that it is not we but Christ who qualifies us and has paid the price for our membership within God's new kingdom through his death on the cross.

What we need to consider now is the difference between our 'access' to God as Christians and the dynamic / relationship that exists between others outside of Christ and God?

How is their relationship with God different from ours?

Firstly, to suggest that no-one outside of the Christian experience of spirituality has any access to God at all would suggest that God is completely absent from the world outside of the Church. This, frankly, seems unimaginable. To suggest that God simply ignores those who respond to him through other religions seems somewhat unlikely especially considering that he is a God of Love whose aim is to embrace his creation on as deeper level as possible. *(see our chapter on judgment above)*

What does appear obvious to me, however, from all the biblical evidence is that there is an unquestionable uniqueness to our relationship with God as the Church 'in Christ'. This sets our experience of God in Jesus apart from anything else which could possibly be attained through any other religious experience. This is clearly evident not only within the teaching of the NT but also within the common experience of Christians, ever since the day of Pentecost. *(see our chapter on the Holy Spirit above)*

Access to God's presence within the Church is therefore indeed uniquely different both to that which had been experienced by anyone prior to the birth of the Church at Pentecost and to any experience of spirituality that might be gleaned from other religions and philosophies outside the Church. It is different because the access to God which Christ brings comes as a result of the indwelling of God's Spirit within the very being of the Christian believer. When we come to Christ in penitence and faith Christ's Holy Spirit joins with us so we become intimately linked to the Father in heaven. All the barriers are taken away so that we can approach the throne of grace with confidence. God becomes literally and spiritually a part of us, we experience his presence in this most intimate of ways. This biblically speaking, is an experience unique only to those 'in Christ'.

This unique relationship was expected within the Old Testament.
Jeremiah 31: 34

"No longer will they teach their neighbour, or say to one another, 'Know the LORD,' because they will all know me, from the least of them to the greatest, For I will forgive their wickedness and will remember their sins no more."

It was promised by Jesus to his disciple's.
John 14 vs 16

16 And I will ask the Father, and he will give you another advocate to help you and be with you forever— 17 the Spirit of truth. The world cannot accept him, because it neither sees him nor knows him. But you know him, for he lives with you and will be in you.

It was fulfilled at Pentecost.
Acts chapter 2 vs 14

14 Then Peter stood up with the Eleven, raised his voice and addressed the crowd: "Fellow Jews and all of you who live in Jerusalem, let me explain this to you; listen carefully to what I say. these people are not drunk, as you suppose. It's only nine in the morning! No, this is what was spoken by the prophet Joel:

'In the last days, God says, I will pour out my Spirit on all people. Your sons and daughters will prophesy, your young men will see visions, your old men will dream dreams. Even on my servants, both men and women, I will pour out my Spirit in those days, and they will prophesy.'

What we have is a unique access to God because of Christ through the giving of his Spirit to the Church.

There are some wonderful consequences in our decision to accept Christ. Conversely, however, bad decisions or a failure to make a right decision can have, as I mentioned at the beginning of this chapter, consequences as well. What if we haven't chosen Christ, what then? Well, I suppose without being too morbid, at the very least it seems obvious to say that we won't discover the opportunity to experience everything we have just talked about! If our experience is to be consistent and if God is to be true to his word, then it follows as obviously as day follows night that if we don't choose to accept Christ then we won't appropriate these incredible blessings. We will not find ourselves at peace with God and God will not be at peace with us. We will not experience this intimate access to God because we will not have accessed his grace and his Spirit will not be poured out upon us! We will not be able to experience any assurance of our eternal life.

Everything we do and every decision we make brings with it its own consequences and those generally like for like: why should the decision of faith then be any different?

Chapter 16

The Pathology of Self destruction

In order to bring this rather poor man's book to a close I thought I would finish back where I started with some final thoughts on the topic of our 'Life Scripts'. The topic of my last chapter attempts to discuss what I would describe as the 'Biggie' of all scripts.

I hope very much that what I have written has been of some interest; a little educational but most of all thought provoking. I hope that I have injected some common sense into the topics that I have tried to discuss and made the theology relevant to some at least. It is my humble opinion that above all else theology should promote the positive qualities of healing, self-worth and hope. This is why Jesus came. The Gospel's key themes are redemption, restoration and love and this is what we should be about if we are to reflect the Love of God within our ministry and within our lives.

So, the final chapter:

I have, throughout my adult life both as a Police Officer and as a Priest, observed within a significant number of people what I describe here in my chapter title as the 'Pathology of Self destruction'. By this I mean an uncontrollable and overpowering determination within certain people's subconscious minds to damage the positive quality of their lives. Time and time again I have seen this pathology at work, to a greater or lesser extent, creeping into the behaviour of those to whom I minister and be-friend.

Somehow, and for some reason, certain people will consistently set themselves on paths which are almost guaranteed to either, prevent them from achieving or having *almost* succeeded, produce failure in the end. Or having succeeded already will inevitably threaten or destroy their own particular success. It is as if such people don't really want to succeed, even though they say that they do, try to and seem for a time to enjoy their success. That is if indeed they survive their own pathology long enough to succeed at all. Such people don't seem to *recognise* themselves *as themselves* when *in success,* as if 'being a success' is not *who they are* or where *they live* psychologically. They don't seem to be able to identify with *that* person; they can't quite cope with being *that* person and so in the end they sabotage their lives. Conversely, they do *recognise* themselves (subconsciously that is) as one who fails, their *self-identity is that of the victim!* Deep down something within their own psychology makes them believe that failure is where they *belong* and as such, they develop the *need to fail* in order to *be themselves.*

Why this should be the case, of course, is different for each individual and stems naturally from deep emotional needs and from a damaged emotional psychology. The most common threads being, perhaps, a lack of self worth, or even a deep-seated hatred of the self. They hold feelings of inadequacy, unworthiness, rejection, abandonment, and have experienced, normally, a lack of love within their lives. This we know fundamentally diminishes the value that one subconsciously places upon oneself. It is probably fair to assume that most of these pathologies would have been implanted into the person's psyche during their early childhood and teenage years, and / or from a significant trauma. Sometimes from a variety of different sources.

This 'pathology of self-destruction' can also have different degrees of influence (power) within people's lives and take on a variety of different forms. The most extreme being such conditions as anorexia, alcoholism, workaholic type behaviour and drug abuse. Lesser negative consequences could be such things as, self-absorption, depression, selfishness, dishonesty, lack of self-worth or over competitiveness. One can also exhibit this pathology through acts of omission as well, by not completing, for example, the work one should do to achieve a success.

The way the pathology affects people's lives can vary in severity and the means by which one can carry out one's own demise are also varied and perhaps too numerous to list. Some examples might help to clarify my thoughts:

A) 'A' is a married man with a lovely caring wife, with children who adore him. 'A', however, is also a workaholic. He spends far too much time consumed with his work. He is also overly ambitious seeking always to impress his senior colleagues. 'A', neglects his family, and despite the pleas of his wife, whom he does actually love, is incapable of developing a balanced lifestyle. As the marriage begins to suffer 'A', blames his wife claiming that she *'doesn't understand him'.* He begins to suffer from the loneliness and lack of affection (sex) that his own lifestyle creates within his marriage. He becomes close to a female colleague and starts an affair. He leaves messages from this female colleague on his phone and the inevitable happens. His wife discovers the betrayal and the separation and divorce that follows causes untold damage to both his, his wife's, and his children's lives.

B) 'B' is a young female teenager who enters foster care. She gets placed in a marvellous home with loving adults who wish to treat her as their own child. She receives all the attention she could ever wish for. she is supported and has the foundation to work towards success and the prospect of a lifetime of support. 'B' turns against the wife of the foster carers and creates an atmosphere so difficult that she has to leave.

In each of these cases 'A' and 'B' demonstrate a compulsion to fail and to destroy all that they have achieved. 'A' could simply have moderated his lifestyle to make sure that he spent the right amount of time with his family, avoid the affair, and once in the affair keep better care of his phone messages and arrangements so that the affair wasn't discovered!

'B' is simply unable to live in this atmosphere of acceptance and love.

In each case, there is, it would seem, a subconscious and pernicious pathology at work. Each individual is being <u>driven</u> by a subconscious and negative life script or scripts which, in turn, makes them prone to unwise behaviour and drives them to jeopardise their prosperity.

Somewhere within their subconscious something whispers, perhaps, that *they are just not worthy,* or they are *never good enough* or they must *always be better,* they *must be the victim* and *'the traumatised' or the 'less than successful'*. And as such their lives sit precariously on, the precipice of tragedy and trauma.

Some examples of these subconscious scripts could sound something like this.

- "I just don't deserve to be successful".

- "I am really unlovable".

- "I am not worth very much".

- "I deserve to be alone".

- "I am never going to be good enough to be loved for who I am".

- "They don't really care for me; they're just pretending".

- "I will only have true 'value' when I am better than everyone else".

Such messages run in the background of our minds on a quiet, almost unintelligible tape whispering their poison into our lives determining how we secretly see ourselves. In most cases without us even realising it. We hear the quiet whispers from our childhood when perhaps Daddy didn't love us as much as we hoped; or mummy told us to just 'shut up'; or when we cried, needed some help but it didn't come. When our parents were disappointed or pushed us to hard to succeed, so hard in fact that nothing ever seemed ever good enough. When we felt undervalued. When our friends teased us at school for being different: When we never felt pretty enough: When we were always picked last for the sports team: When the teacher told us, we were stupid. When we suffered a particular trauma, which left us forever scarred within.

The list of 'triggers' goes on and on. Some say even back to experiences within the womb. Unless we have been very lucky in our lives it is a fact that most of us, with a little self-reflection, would probably recognise some of these influences within our own lives. We are all, I suspect, damaged goods to some extent or another.

In my own background there have been some quite significant opportunities for such negative scripts to become influential in my life. I came from a 'broken home', my Mother was a paranoid schizophrenic who also (if that wasn't enough) suffered from manic depression. I lived as a teenager in nothing less than domestic chaos and spent the vast majority of my time, from aged 15 onwards, anywhere but at home. I lacked much of the parental love and support that I should have had as my parents battled to unsuccessfully save their own marriage, and to be fair, survive the pressures of their own lives.

I compensated through two things; girls and the Church, through which I managed to find much of the love and family that I was naturally missing. I was almost adopted by my Church youth leaders without whose love, support and home, I would not be the person I, thankfully, became in the end.

Which brings me nicely to the answer and to my point.

Of all the life scripts I have written about, this 'pathology of self destruction' is, in my experience, the most powerful of them all it's like the **'Super Script'** because when it kicks in it pulls all the other scripts together into a cocktail of utter destruction. We can have *some* life scripts, and let's face it most of us do, which can be inconvenient and which can cause some pain or prevent the enhancement of some joy. This one when in full flow, is an unstoppable train which derails the entire quality of life. It can lead to utter devastation and even to suicide and achieve all that without the victim even knowing it is there. There is only one answer, only one hope, only one strategy which can offer any prospect of deliverance. Namely a combination of *honest confrontation and unconditional love.*

Many counselling and pastoral techniques concentrate on simply reflecting and affirming one of the most 'in vogue' examples of such has currently been re-branded as 'talk therapy'. Such practices, in my humble experience are woefully inadequate when faced with this beast because they refuse to challenge. Listening is simply not enough to treat this animal. It must be identified and sacrificed, the person must be embraced, in as much love as it is possible to give. Only then can healing come. Within the Christian context, this means that our theology, our preaching, our pastoral care and our teaching must, if we are to bring God's grace into such people's lives, rise to this challenge. We must get the message of God's grace right for this is the corruption of sin at its most influential, the influence of Satan at its peak. This is our holy war.

To take us right back to the beginning of this book we must forsake the infectious nonsensical pseudo biblical trash so often promoted through poor teaching and quick fix Christian books and we must 'DO' Theology well.

Woe betides any minister or priest whose message of the Gospel re-enforces such damaging negative influences within people's lives. As our Lord warned *"If you cause even one of my little ones to fall it would better that you had a rock placed around your neck and be thrown into the sea"*

I am, in the end, not sure how well this small offering will be received. I hope it will be of some interest. As I said in the beginning, I think I have something to say. It is offered with passion and in response to those I love whose pain I have seen and into whose lives I have tried, however failingly, to minister the almighty love and grace of God in Christ.

With much love David.

For more information contact:

Rev'd David W. John
info@advbooks.com

To purchase additional copies of these books, visit our bookstore
at: www.advbookstore.com

Longwood, Florida, USA
"we bring dreams to life" ™
www.advbookstore.com

Lightning Source UK Ltd.
Milton Keynes UK
UKHW022230090421
381737UK00008B/339